T0208193

Marcien Towa's African Philosophy:
Two Texts

Translated and Introduced
by
Tsenay Serequeberhan

Hdri Publishers
Asmara
2012

Hdri Publishers
178 Tegadelti Street
House No.35
P.O. Box 1081
Tel. 291-1-126177
Fax 291-1-125630
Asmara, Eritrea

L'idée d'une philosophie négro-africaine by Marcien Towa
Copyright © 1979 Les Editions Clé

Propositions sur l'identité culturelle by Marcien Towa
© Revue Présence Africaine, n° 109, 1979

Translated and Introduced by Tsenay Serequeberhan (Ph.D.)
ISBN 99948-0-049-3

Cover art: Tesfa-Alem Atenaw

Printed in Eritrea by Sabur Printing Services

All proceeds from the sale of this short book will be donated to *The Eritrean National War Disabled Veterans Association* (ENWDVA).

Table of Contents

Acknowledgements

L'idee d'une philosophie négro-africaine published in 1979 by *Editions CLE, Yaoundé, Cameroun* and *"Propositions sur l'identité culturelle"* published in *Présence Africaine*, No. 109, 1st Quarter, 1979. I also would like to thank and acknowledge the many students of French who, over many years, helped me in making the translation of these two texts possible. Finally, I thank and acknowledge Tsigye Haile-Michael who very graciously agreed to look-over substantial chunks of the final draft and generously made available to me her knowledge and understanding of the French language. Any flaws or errors that may remain, as is always the case in such matters, are my sole responsibility.

I

A Note on Translation

A translation has to aim at rendering the meaning of a text without compromising its self-presentation. To understand/interpret a text, especially in philosophy, one has to come to terms with the *manner* in which it is articulated. For, in philosophy, the *style* and/or *manner* of presentation is not, and can never be, an external ornament.

Heraclitus's curt sayings, Socrates's dialogical manner, the pregnant aphorisms of Nietzsche (and one could go on and on with many more examples), are themselves organic components of the *sense* that these thinkers are trying to convey. The substance of their thought shows itself, or comes forth, in and through the manner in which it is expressed. Thus, language is not – in these, as in all other cases – a neutral instrument, receptacle, and/or extrinsic medium.

Between *sense* and *style* one should always opt for the former, while stubbornly trying to stay, as much as possible, true to the latter. To diverge "too much" from the *style* is to compromise the very *sense*, or meaning, one is trying to put across. For, the challenge of translation is to relocate or carry-over, from one language into another, that which has been expressed and, as much as possible, in *the manner* in which it has been expressed. To paraphrase, in other words, is not to translate.

In this regard, it has to be emphasized that, along with recognizing the difficulties of translation one should also acknowledge its concrete possibility. As Antonio Gramsci puts it, "A great culture can be translated into the language of another great culture, that is to say a great national language with historic richness and complexity, and it can translate any other great culture and can be a world-wide means of expression. But a dialect cannot do this."[1] Thus, with all of its attendant risks and difficulties, accurate translation is "tricky" but indeed possible. Here, "accurate translation" refers to the fidelity of interpretation internal to the understanding which informs and constitutes a translation. Accuracy hinges on an awareness of the interpretative character of all translation. It is the translator who is conscious of this, and what it calls for, that can properly put his or her conscious self-awareness in the service of the daunting task of translation.

One last point, Towa's *Biblical* and *Qu'ranic* citations have not been modified. In most cases they varied,

---

[1]   Antonio Gramsci, *Prison Notebooks*, edited and introduced by Quintin Hoare and Geoffrey Nowell Smith (New York: International Publishers, 1992), p. 325.

slightly, from the versions of these religious texts available to me in English. The variations, however, were not such as to affect the tenor, substance, and/or character of the arguments in question. In like manner, and for similar reasons, I have also left the Pharaonic-Egyptian texts as given by Towa.

Finally, from time to time, I have utilized square brackets [ ] to insert explanatory footnotes and, in the body of the text, English that in the French is implicit or to retain French words whose meaning is rendered, but not quite, by the English that translates them. Alas, the text is at times awkward! The reader's kind indulgence is therefore gently requested in the recognition that the sacrifice of elegance, in favor of substance, is an offering rendered on the high and ancient altar of *Hermes* when one undertakes the daunting task of translation. For, as Plato noted long ago, "All great things are risky and, as the saying goes, what is beautiful is difficult."[2]

---

[2] *Plato's Republic*, translated by G.M.A. Grube (Indianapolis, IN: Hackett Pub., 1982), p. 153, #497e.

II

Translator's Introduction

Next, said Socrates, I believe that it [the earth] is vast in size, and that we who dwell between the river Phasis and the Pillars of Hercules inhabit only a minute portion of it – we live round the sea like ants or frogs round a pond – and there are many other peoples inhabiting similar regions.

Plato[3]

How are we to know in advance what insights and what understanding and self-understanding the experience of what has come down to us will lead to, and indeed this includes what has come down to us from world cultures, not just the European! Indeed, we...need to accept our worldwide heritage not only in its otherness but also in recognizing the validity of the claim this larger heritage makes on us.

Hans-Georg Gadamer[4]

The Idea of a Negro-African Philosophy is a short book

---

[3] Edith Hamilton and Huntington Cairns *Plato Collected Dialogues*, "Phaedo" translated by Hugh Tredennick (Princeton, NJ: Princeton University Press, 1989), p. 90, #109b.

[4] *Gadamer in Conversation*, edited and translated by Richard E. Palmer (New Haven & London: Yale University Press, 2001), p. 54.

originally published in 1979. It is a concise, yet thorough and systematic, exploration of the question of African philosophy as it emerges out of the central concerns of our postcolonial present. *"Propositions on Cultural Identity"* a short article, published in the same year, is a succinct philosophic exploration of the question of identity, as it pertains to the cultural, political, and economic issues linked to Africa's politico-economic dependence on the West.

In both texts – presented here in translation for the first time – Towa engages the question of African philosophy by concretely exploring and showing how this question is organically linked to the efforts of the Continent aimed at reclaiming its economic, political, historical, and existential actuality. Broaching the question from slightly differing, yet complimentary, angles Towa articulates a stance that directly engages the central concerns of African independence, in the context of a postcolonial world that is still *tied* to the apron-strings of its former colonizers.

For him, it is the complicated folds and creases of this simple, but knotted, *tie* that must be concretely – i.e., politically – un-knotted if Africa is truly to become independent. He is focused, in these two texts, on philosophically exploring the avenues for consummating this worthwhile project. What we have, in other words, is the articulation of a stance responsive to the fundamental concerns of our postcolonial present.

Thus, the Anglophone reader – participant and/or

audience – of the contemporary discourse of African philosophy has in hand, for the first time, the substantial views, on African philosophy, of a neglected major figure. And unlike the opinions, regarding his work, circulated and popularized by Abiola Irele, Kwame Anthony Appiah, and D.A. Masolo, Towa does not share Paulin J. Hountondji's outlook, nor does he espouse a Eurocentric perspective.[5] He holds a view that is critical and yet sympathetically inclined towards the African past, in the context of present concerns. This is a view/stance that is cognizant of its past in being open to the concrete possibilities of its future. Describing a similar perspective, from within the context of enslavement and the struggle against it, Frederick Douglass writes: "We have to do with the past only as we can make it useful to the present and to the future. To all inspiring motives, to noble deeds which can be gained from the past, we are welcome."[6] Towa's position is a specification of this critical and, at the same time, receptive attitude to the past from within the

---

[5] For Irele see the introduction to, *African Philosophy Myth and Reality* (Bloomington, IN: Indiana University Press, 1983) and specifically, pp. 25 – 26; for Appiah see, *In My Father's House* (New York: Oxford University Press, 1992), p. 95; and for Masolo see, *African Philosophy in Search of Identity* (Bloomington, IN: Indiana University Press, 1994), pp. 164 – 178.

[6] Frederick Douglass, "What to the Slave is the Fourth of July," in *Narrative of the Life of Frederick Douglass an American Slave Written by Himself*, Part Two, "Selected Reviews, Documents and Speeches," edited with an introduction by David W. Blight (Boston, MA: Bedford/St. Martin's, 2003), p. 154.

concerns of the present.

Thus, reflecting on the intellectual productions of this present, and specifically focusing on Hountondji, Towa writes: "The Current of thought represented by P. Hountondji does not occlude African thought, it openly excludes it in the name of scientificity, as not in the least pertinent. For this author there is no African philosophy in the traditional culture and there could not be one."[7] This view, for Towa, is tantamount to "turning our backs on our ancestors."[8] Commenting further, on Hountondji's position, he states: "The immediate consequence of this will be that Africans...with the responsibility of teaching philosophy will turn away from works of the spirit [works of the mind] produced by Africans for thousands of years. I do not see what we stand to gain from such...amnesia, not even to consider the thought of our ancestors as worthy of being examined and discussed."[9] These quotations – taken from an article published in French in 1981 and available in English since 1991 – evidence Towa's categorical rejection of Hountondji's position. And they show him to be favorably disposed to the intellectual productions of pre-colonial/traditional Africa.

---

[7] Marcien Towa, "Conditions for the Affirmation of a Modern African Philosophical Thought," in *African Philosophy: The Essential Readings*, edited and introduced by Tsenay Serequeberhan (New York: Paragon House, 1991), p. 191.
[8] Ibid. p. 192.
[9] Ibid. p. 195.

His stance towards "our ancestors" – or the "works of the spirit…produced by Africans for thousands of years" – is not dismissive but critically sympathetic. According to Towa, our traditions have to be critically scrutinized and systematically sifted in view of the concerns and exigencies of the present.[10] In all of this, for him, the proper task of philosophy is to identify and minister to the core problems of its time – its history. Or, as he puts it: "In this sense, African philosophy is the exercise by Africans of a specific type of intellectual activity (the critical examination of fundamental problems) applied to African reality. The type of intellectual activity in question is, as such, neither African, European, Greek, nor German; it is philosophy in general."[11] Thus, the term "African philosophy" is a designation for this "type of intellectual activity" as it unfolds out of the horizon/ambient (i.e., the concerns and issues) of contemporary Africa.

Towa gives voice to a stance that can best be described as a radically engaged and praxis oriented philosophy focused on the socio-political transformation of the Continent, aimed at reclaiming the dashed hopes of Africa's independence struggle. A stance focused on the possibility of African freedom, beyond our postcolonial malaise. And unlike Hountondji, or Appiah, Towa holds the view that we need to critically explore our traditional – intellectual and cultural – resources in tandem with, and by

[10] Ibid. pp. 193 – 198.
[11] Ibid. p. 195.

way of engaging, the concerns of the present. In this hermeneutic of liberation the function of philosophy is to persuade, clarify, and in so doing engage, the historico-political problems of the present in view of fashioning a desirable future: a future that would be tailor-fitted to those who have been, thus far, the victims of African independence – the vast majority, perpetually condemned to economic destitution and political insignificance.[12] In other words:

> All post-colonial societies are still subject in one way or another to overt or subtle forms of neo-colonial domination, and independence has not solved this problem. The development of new elites within independent societies, often buttressed by neo-colonial institutions; the development of internal divisions based on racial, linguistic or religious discriminations; the continuing unequal treatment of indigenous peoples in settler/invader societies – all these testify to the fact that post-colonialism is a continuing process of resistance and reconstruction.[13]

In this respect, it can be said that, Towa consciously articulates a perspective that concretely engages the issues and concerns of the dispossessed vast majority. The

---

[12] See what Appiah says of this segment of African society in, *In My Father's House*, chapter, 8.

[13] *The Post-Colonial Studies Reader, Second Edition*, edited by Bill Ashcroft, Gareth Griffiths, and Helen Tiffin (New York: Routledge, 2006), pp. 1 – 2.

concerns of the Africa that, in its victory over colonialism, was defeated by the residues of the past it had overcome. This then is the radical stance, rooted in the dashed hopes of the anti-colonial struggle, which Towa concretely gives voice to. A stance aimed at thinking and furthering the "continuing process of resistance and reconstruction."

Still, one could ask: What is the value of these texts, now thirty and some years old, for the contemporary discourse of African philosophy? The short answer to this question: Towa is timely and relevant! One need only flip through these pages to verify this assertion. Having done so, each reader will have to decide for him/her self the value and pertinence of these texts.

For the rest, as Hegel noted long ago, *prefaces* and/or *introductions* in philosophy, are of limited value. It is *der Sache selbst*, "the thing itself," which has to establish and/or impose its claim on its audience. As the reader will soon find out Towa is an imposing, majestic, and timely writer/thinker, as relevant today as thirty years ago.

Tsenay Serequeberhan
Asmara, Eritrea
June, 2012

III

The Idea of a Negro-African Philosophy

Detailed Table of Contents

INTRODUCTION

The theme that was proposed to us, "the problematic of a Negro-African philosophy," confirms the awakening of modern Africa, and of the black world, to philosophic consciousness.[14] It also allows us to think that philosophy,

----

[14] The theme of this text was proposed to us for the Festival of Lagos where it was to be presented in the form of a public conference. Unable, for reasons beyond our control, to go to Lagos, we have given our text a greater development. We have also changed the initial title, *"La problématique d'une philosophie négro-africaine"* replacing it by that which you have in front of your eyes, in order to avoid confusion with our *"Essai sur la problématique philosophique dans l'Afrique*

that is to say, the conceptual debate on our essential problems, is on the way to becoming one of the major modes of expression of contemporary Africa. Such an evolution would indicate that the dismal epoch in the course of which Africa was nothing more than a field of invasions, not only military but also ideological, is headed towards its termination and an era is opening in which our continent will participate again in the elaboration of global thought.

To avoid the ethnophilosophic pitfall one must expressly underline this truism: a Negro-African philosophy is a philosophy; different philosophies can very well be particular and also divergent, but they are nonetheless all philosophies. This observation places us in front of a specific case of the general problem of the *one* and the *many*. To set aside this difficulty – because it is indeed a difficulty – with a slight-of-hand on some pretext or other, is to run the risk of speaking without saying anything; for "knowledge" of the undefined, pure indeterminacy, is pure nothing [i.e., no knowledge at all]. I don't see how one can avoid this empty and confused *logomachy* [semantic dispute] without recourse to a classical procedure: indicate that which philosophy is in general or at least that which one intends by it, demonstrate thereafter how different philosophies are articulated interior to this conception of philosophy, and then go on to focus attention on the problems that call for

actuelle" (Yaoundé, Cameroun: Editions CLE, 1971).

the elaboration of a contemporary Negro-African philosophy responsive to our aspirations and our actual needs.

I. PHILOSOPHY AND ITS PROBLEMS

In what follows we will present a preliminary delimitation of the domain of philosophy in general, simply to indicate of what we are speaking. Without such a procedure we run the risk of engaging in a dialogue of the deaf.

1 –Philosophy as the Thought of the Absolute

Philosophy exists. It presents itself as a collection of works said to be philosophical. The reading of these works imposes, it seems to us, the idea that philosophy is the courage to think the absolute. The human being thinks, and, of all *known* beings, it is the only one that thinks. Thought is here understood in a restrictive sense: in the sense of weighing, discussing representations, beliefs, opinions, confronting them, examining the pros and cons of each, selecting critically, in order to retain only that which can stand-up to the test of criticism and classification. In this restrictive sense, representations, convictions, opinions that have not endured the test of criticism, or have not survived it, are not thoughts or ideas properly speaking but simple beliefs. In daily life, all adult and sane human beings are capable of thought; all human beings can engage in a discussion of representations on current opinions concerning practical, theoretic, or esthetic matters of quotidian life.

But certain domains of human life, and precisely the most important, try to escape from all scrutiny, from all discussion and critique, that is to say, from thought. This is generally the case of religion and of [political] power. Every society, every collectivity organizes its activities and its comportment in view of certain fundamental objectives, of certain essential values and conforms to certain norms that are imposed on everything. Values and norms that are supreme derive their absolute authority from a conception of the world acknowledged by the society or from a recital of primordial eventuations, cosmic and epic, which have given birth to the established social order and on which it is based. The heroes of these eventuations are Gods, or in all cases, beings gifted with faculties and powers superior to those of normal human beings. This amounts to saying that values and norms rest on myths, on sacred recitals whose heroes are beings that are, more or less, supernatural. The Enuma Elish, the great Akkadian myth of creation, recounts the war of Mardouk against Tiamat. After the victory over his enemies, Mardouk immolates Kingou, the chief of the armies of the Gods who supported Tiamat. From his blood, he creates humanity and imposes on it the service to the Gods in order to release the inferior

Gods from this labor. Another Akkadian text enumerates the diverse labors, the various occupations that are to be the lot of humanity: the great labor of construction, of canalization, of agriculture, of animal-husbandry, craftsmanship, etc. The deity has determined the destiny of each: "Specialist after specialist, laborer after laborer, like grain, they themselves will sprout in the sun, a fact that will no more change henceforth than the stars in the sky.

> Day and Night
> To accomplish the feasts/celebrations of the gods
> They (the gods) have themselves decided
> These grand designs..."[15]

The human being is a slave of the Gods and of their terrestrial representatives, that is to say, a slave to [political] power. That which pertains to him in his existence is imposed on him by the Gods. There is nothing to refuse or to discuss in that which is ordered by the divinity. In the *Genesis* of the Yahwist's [i.e., the Hebrews], we find this same conception of the human being. He is here presented as the farmer of God: "Yahweh thus took man and placed him in the Garden of Eden in order for him to work it and guard it" with the interdiction regarding the eating of the fruit of "the-tree-of-the-discernment-of-good-and-evil." From the point of view of myth, to want to judge good and evil for oneself, is

---

[15] *La naissance du monde*, Seuil, p. 150. [No other source or reference specification has been given.]

absolute evil. This is why the [book of] *Genesis*, of the Yahwist's, attributes such a project to the Devil himself.

Now, to develop thought so that it becomes the measure for the discernment of good and evil and [in this manner] assume [responsibility for] the direction of one's life, this is precisely the project of philosophy. And that is why there is between it [i.e., philosophy] and myth a profound opposition. This opposition is the subject of one of the early dialogues of Plato, *Euthyphro*; Euthyphro is a young diviner. To Socrates's question, what is piety, what is religion, he responds: "Piety, I would say, is that which I am about to do. Whether it concerns murder or sacrilegious theft or any other act of the same sort, piety consists in pursuing the culprit, father, mother or whoever, it does not matter; not to do so, there you have impiety."[16] The proof, for Euthyphro, is that Zeus, the best and the most just of the Gods chained his father Kronos because he [i.e., Kronos] unjustly devoured his own children. Kronos himself had inflicted on his father a similar treatment. But Euthyphro does not respond to the question of Socrates. The question of Socrates leads to the proper nature, the essence of piety in general and not to what someone, man or God, wants, does, likes or approves. Only a general definition of piety can serve as a criterion

---

[16] Platon, *Euthyphron*, société d'édition "Belle Letters," p. 189. [*Plato, Five Dialogues, Euthyphro, Apology, Crito, Meno, Phaedo*, trans., by G.M.A. Grube (Indianapolis, IN: Hackett Pub., 1981), 5e, p. 9.]

for determining, in each case, that which is pious and that which is not. The mythical mentality erects directly an individual comportment as a universal norm of comportment, an individual opinion as a universal truth, merely from the fact that it has to do with the comportment, the will, or the declarations of an individual, man or God, which is taken as exemplary. That which a mythical spirit takes as a norm of thought or of conduct is in fact the exceptional and exemplary individual, the great man, chief, hero or God. In the domain of thought as in that of conduct, it always submits, out of admiration, out of love, or, in most cases, out of fear, to an exterior authority. The cult of personality, the blind submission to some great personality constitutes the fundamental characteristics of the mythical mentality. All problems, practical or theoretic, pertaining to the absolute are resolved by reference to what another wants or thinks, an extraordinary personality, real or imagined, still living or having lived "*in illo tempore*" whose will constitutes law and whose opinion is the truth, myths are the narratives of such gestures. That which thus essentially characterizes a mythical spirit is its inability or its renunciation of thought, of reflecting in a personal and an autonomous manner – I did not say solitary – in order to "discern good and evil," in order to find that which has to be admitted as true or as the norm of comportment. It [i.e., the mythical mentality] unloads this responsibility on another: a mythical hero, a "great man," a charismatic chief, a God, etc...

Now, this confidence conferred on the Gods is not well placed, since among the Gods, among religions, just as among men, are to be found the same conflicts and the same disagreements on the same issues. Among the Gods, as among religions, conflicts and wars arise from these same issues: the just and the unjust, good and evil, truth and lies [falsehood] or error, in modern terms, the question of "values." And so, the solution to our problems is not to be found in the sky, in the hands of Gods or charismatic chiefs, providential men and other saviors. To expect from them a response to our theoretic interrogations and our practical hesitations is to flee the necessary effort of reflection, of personal thought, through discussion and methodic research. The opposition between myth and the idea [of philosophy] reverts to the opposition between received opinion and active thought. Myth is an invitation to the wonder struck divagation of the spirit across time and space. Philosophy refuses such vagabondism in imaginary countries and, to the faith of the devout, it opposes doubt, incredulity. But in the eyes of the devout, philosophic incredulity is impiety which it stigmatizes as "disbelief"; doubt is diabolic, the "unbeliever" has a pact with evil. In reality in refusing to naïvely lend credence to mythological fantasies, philosophy does not declare war on the good, it only wants to [critically] think mythological beliefs, that is to say to grasp the ensemble in view of the spirit [or the idea of philosophy], to weigh and ponder in order to determine their truth value, it refuses to deliver human beings bound hand and foot to tyranny, enemy of liberty and thus also of thought.

2 –The Practical Dimension of Philosophy

If one admits that philosophy is before all else a refusal of the principle of authority in any domain and that this is a requirement of rationality, one must also agree then that it rests [or is grounded] on the same foundation as science. Between philosophy and religious dogmatism or the despotism which it habitually serves, there is a frank opposition. But between philosophy and science, there simply is a distinction to be made. Science is characterized by a narrow specialization, the concern for ethical and ideological neutrality and the requirement of a more rigorous [and narrow] verification of its results. The expert in order to sufficiently dominate his subject specializes very narrowly. He thereby also deprives himself of the possibility of speaking, as an expert, on the direction that society ought to take and the norms that it should adopt to this effect. For him to be in a position to do so, to pronounce [i.e., speak] on the absolute, he must have a more general view of reality as a whole. By depriving himself, due to his restrictive specialization and by reason of his ethical neutrality, of the right to pronounce on the ultimate ends of society, he renounces the use, as an expert, of the human faculty for the discernment of good and evil; modern experts [in this manner] leave the hands of politicians and Churches free to impose arbitrarily and in an authoritarian manner on humanity laws and ethical directives which are based on nothing more than the fantasy of myth and blind passions. Philosophy on the contrary intends to intervene in all the debates concerned with the destiny of humanity. Whereas the politician essentially counts on force and constraint to bend human beings to his will, whereas the Churches, appealing to myths, aim to rouse the sensibility and inflame the imagination, philosophy aims at that which is the most elevated in the human being: thought. Most certainly, philosophy cannot dream of mastering all the sciences. It can nonetheless acquire a view of reality as a whole by interrogating the principal sciences as to their objectives, their methods, and the main results thus obtained. The knowledge of reality acquired in this manner, associated with great intellectual rigor, allows philosophy to intervene with authority in the search for the ultimate meaning to be given to our efforts and to the essential norms of comportment.

3 – Philosophy and Philosophies

The philosophical path is characterized, we say, by the intimate liaison [i.e., connection] between the concern to know rationally, methodically, physical as well as socio-cultural reality and the will to rely on this knowledge to define the most important and ultimate orientation that should be adopted in human comportment [*comportement humain*]. Human beings act in view of satisfying their needs and aspirations. Now reality is varied in its situations and thus poses to human beings problems that are different in accordance with these situations. Needs and aspirations vary in consequence. The more human beings are active and the more they transform the environment [*le milieu*], they themselves are transformed in their needs and aspirations. In the end, the opposition between classes and peoples rests on opposing interests and aspirations, such that reality is not considered in the same perspective or in the same light. The differences and oppositions that affect reality and the interests they drag along, of differences and oppositions, correspond in their theoretic expression [to differing philosophic positions] and lead to different and even to opposing philosophies. However, whatever their divergences, all philosophies in order to merit the name philosophy, must result from a debate on the absolute, on reality, on values, and on the highest norms.

II. AFRICAN PHILOSOPHY, MYTH OR REALITY

To admit the existence of multiple philosophies is to accept the possibility of a particular African philosophy.

To circumscribe, to delimit within culture in general, the particular domain of philosophy in opposition to that of myth and to distinguish it from science and from other components [or areas] of culture, is to let it be understood that the possibility of an African philosophy is conditional.

1 – Is There A Negro African Philosophy Properly Speaking?

The question of the existence or nonexistence of a properly African philosophy is not susceptible to an intelligible response except on one condition: that those who pose it are from the start in accord on what they mean by philosophy. Ask him who doesn't have an idea if "*evu*" exists, and you will infallibly elicit the preliminary question: what is this which is *evu*? African society is it endogamic, totemism does it exist in Africa? One cannot respond sensibly to these questions if one does not know, to begin with, that which ethnologists name endogamy or totemism. Socialism, feudalism, democracy, do they exist in Africa? The response presupposes that he who is to respond has a sufficiently specified idea of socialism, feudalism, and of democracy. Now it is quite clear that if I want to acquire serious knowledge of totemism, [or] of political systems, it is to those who study these questions that I will address myself, unless I force myself to study them on my own. In any case, it is necessary to reflect on what totemism, socialism, capitalism, etc., might be, since it is not easy to come to an understanding of what they are. The same is true for the question of the existence or nonexistence of a properly African philosophy. It presupposes the response to the question: what is this which is philosophy? A formidable question that many avoid asking, but which cannot be evaded, otherwise, the problem of the existence of an African philosophy will not make any sense.

In order to have an idea of the nature of philosophy one has to start with known philosophic works, interrogate [i.e., examine] these works and the discipline which carries the name philosophy. Now these works are European, their name is European and it is above all in European universities that the discipline called philosophy has been taught for centuries. Noting this is not to affirm that philosophy is exclusively European, even less is it to pronounce on the opportunity to adopt or reject European philosophy. It is simply to seek to discover the reality designated by the word "philosophy." It is only after the reality that Europeans designate, by the word "philosophy," has been grasped that it will be possible to pronounce on its [possible] extension and on its value. But can one discover the reality aimed at by the European word "philosophy," which is equal to circumscribing the domain [of philosophy] and of passing judgment on it, without reading and comprehending the European works when it is a question of this concept [i.e., of philosophy]?

Can one understand these works without reflecting on the problems which they raise, without being involved in philosophy? In other words, in order to really grasp the content of the word "philosophy" and above all to be in a position to pass judgment on this content, it is necessary to become, more or less, philosophers. The path that leads to the meaning of the word philosophy is the way to a spiritual adventure that introduces us to the center of the reality of philosophy. Once we reach this center, we can then know if the ground that we tread is a territory already known to us and experienced from the start, or a "*terra incognita.*" Whether the domain of philosophy is for us a foreign land or a territory with which we are already well acquainted, the question still remains of knowing what judgment to pass on philosophy and what decision to take in its regard.

But, one might object, why take the path of the European word "philosophy" and of European works of philosophy in order to discover (or rediscover) the reality of philosophy? Could we not also start with an African word and with African texts in order to attain the same result?

Theoretically, nothing prevents us from searching for a path of access to the meaning of the word "philosophy" starting from an African language and from African texts. But in fact this path has not been taken, because the question of the existence of an African philosophy did not surge forth from [within] the spontaneous and autonomous developments of African society. We have not inquired among ourselves in order to know if we think philosophically or not, if we have a philosophy or not. We are only trying to give a response to a problem formulated, not by us, but by the ideologues of European imperialism. It is the European philosophers who have formulated the syllogism of racism, the ideological foundation of European imperialism. The syllogism of racism can be enunciated thus:

> The human being is essentially a thinking being, a reasonable being.
> Now the Negro is incapable of thinking and of reasoning. He does not have a philosophy, he has a pre-logical mentality, etc...
> Therefore, the Negro is not really a human being and can be, with good reason, enslaved, and treated like an animal.

Philosophy being, in the eyes of European philosophers, the most brilliant and the highest manifestation of human reason, to deny it to Negros is nothing but the preciseness proper to the minor term in the racist and imperialist syllogism.

It is evident that one does not at all unsettle the syllogism stated above simply by modifying the sense of the word "philosophy" as a number of "African philosophers" have done, who, most often, are in reality nothing more than theologians, prisoners of the mythical mentality (*Biblical* or *Qu'ranic*). To affirm that Africans have a philosophy or their own proper philosophies, but in so doing to revert the meaning of the word philosophy to that of "myth," is not at all to refute the racist syllogism, it is rather to confirm it, to recognize that the African has a pre-logical mentality, and is a stranger to reason. I see two ways of refuting the racist and imperialist reasoning: either by, enlarging the meaning of the word "philosophy" in order to return it to that of myth, in which case it is equally necessary to modify the major term of the [racist] syllogism and to propose a new definition of the human being, to elaborate a new philosophical anthropology: or by preserving in the word philosophy its rational content and demonstrating that Africans have produced such philosophies or, at least, that they are capable of such production.

The choice of one or the other of these solutions is not a question of taste, a subjective preference. What is at stake is to put forth and oppose an efficacious resistance to the ideological mystification of imperialism and of oppression and to avoid all complicity, conscious or unconscious, with domination, because the fate of philosophy is [directly] tied to that of liberty. It seems to us [or], according to us, reason effectively constitutes the essential character of the human being, with which all people are equally gifted, but reason is more or less developed in accordance with the greater or lesser favorable conditions that are offered to it in different social regimes. To admit that discussions directed towards the absolute (that-is-to-say philosophy) assuredly constitute an arduous and dangerous enterprise is to also agree that philosophy is one of the highest manifestations of thought.

2 – *Philosophy and Anti-Philosophy*

All cultures, are they acquainted with the development of philosophic thought? This question, in our opinion, calls for a negative response, since a great number of societies do not tolerate any discussion of beliefs, of values or of their ultimate norms. Not all have philosophy, but all are capable of it. There may not be societies that are entirely strangers to philosophic thought. Those in which philosophic reflection is not manifested seem more anti-philosophical than truly a-philosophical. The culture of the Hebrews, such as it is expressed in the *Bible*, offers a good example of anti-philosophical culture. Hostility to thought is brutally affirmed in the [book of] *Genesis* of the Yahwist's, one of the oldest texts in the entire *Bible*. According to this text, the sin of sins, the original sin of man was to have eaten of the tree of the discernment of good and evil, that is to say, to have dared to think for-himself the ultimate values and norms of his conduct instead of contenting himself with executing the orders of another. Original sin, from the *Biblical* point of view is, in sum, the thought of the absolute, that is to say philosophy.

It is a question of rivalry between master and slave, between God and man and not of an infirmity or of a real inferiority of man to God; this latter [i.e., God] appears here as a fantastic actualization [*réalisation*] of oriental despotism. God himself, according to our myth, recognizes that man is a harassed and stifled being, kept artificially in subordination and not in essence an inferior being, since He makes this acknowledgment: "Behold man has become like one of us, for he knows good and evil!"[17] Centuries later Job will relapse and will want to question the dogma of Providence which, unfailingly, punishes the wicked and rewards the good. He [i.e., Job] did not commit any evil. Why is he made to endure the fate one says is reserved for the wicked, while they prosper? Job believes in the impossibility of engaging in any type of debate with God: "He is not, like me, a man: it is impossible to argue, to appear together before a court of justice, nor is there any arbitration between us..."[18] And in fact, Yahweh intervenes "from the center of the storm" and cuts short all questioning, any inclination that man might have to distinguish between good and evil, by intimidating and terrorizing Job with the display of a power which is, really, nothing more than the determinism of natural elements and of a science that appears to modern humanity as a hymn to the ignorance of a barbaric era. But Job does not have a reply and the threatening words of Yahweh wrest

[17] *Genesis*, 3, 22.
[18] *Job*, 9, 32-33.

from him the avowal of a blind submission and the
renunciation of philosophic thought:

> Yes, I was thoughtless! How could I counter?
> I will put my hand on my mouth!
> I have uttered once! I will not repeat.
> I know that you are all-powerful.
> Because of this I submit myself, repentant,
> in dust and in ashes.[19]

The resignation of thought and submission consecrate
the collapse and humiliation of the human being under the
rod of a God hostile to reason, a God who is nothing but
the transparent disguise of oriental despotism.

The *Qu'ran* takes up again, essentially, the *Biblical*
mythology, but not without aggravating the dogmatism,
the hatred of all discussion and brutality. The *Qu'ran* is
entirely built on the opposition between the believer, the
submissive, the resigned and the non-believer, the rebel.
The believer accepts everything that the Prophet declares
and promises; he humiliates himself, submits and resigns
himself to the unfathomable will of Allah, in the hope of
material rewards in this world and in the beyond. "They
will rest on peaceful beds arranged in order; and we will
unite them with virgins with big dark eyes."[20] "In truth for
those who fear (Allah), there is a journey of happiness,
orchards and vines, virgins with round firm breasts, of an

---

[19] *Job*, 42, 1-5.
[20] *The Qur'an*, Surah 52, 20.

equal age (to theirs) with full cups."[21] The supreme occupation of the believer, the submissive, the resigned, the price he must pay to merit this Epicurean Paradise: humiliate himself, prostrate himself, tremble with fear of and the praise for Allah on his lips in order to exalt His power and His infinite wisdom. And since it must be permitted to doubt the reality of such a crude Paradise and its author, a fancy disguise for a crass oriental despot, the praise and adoration are in fact addressed to the Envoy, to the Prophet, to the spokesman, who is himself quite real and very much alive. It is he who imposes his will, it is he who threatens and crushes the human being, it is he who exercises a discretionary power on the terrorized and resigned masses, it is he who imposes a degrading *griotism* [*le griotisme avilissant*].

As to the non-believer, his only crime is wanting to comprehend, demanding proof before believing, refusing arbitrariness, resignation, prostration, "griotism": in short degradation. The non-believer observes that the self-styled Envoy is "a mortal like one of us." And why "would the warning be given to him alone amongst us all? No! He is an insolent liar."[22] His pretended revelations, continues the non-believer, were taught to him by foreigners. We know what he will say: "It is merely the teaching of a man!" The Prophet replies: "The language of him to whom they allude, is a foreign language, while that of the *Qu'ran* is

---

[21] Ibid. Surah, 78, 31-34.
[22] Ibid. Surah, 54, 23-25.

pure Arabic."[23] Not a very convincing argument. What is certain is that the *Qu'ran* is nothing more than a resumption of the *Bible* starting from some commentaries and adaptations conceived in the spirit of a more intransigent and brutal dogmatism. The story of Joseph, the *Qu'ran* presents it as having been the object of a particularly important revelation to Mohammed. The *Surah* that recounts it ends in this way: "Such is this unknown story (taken from accounts) that We reveal to you. (It is Allah who speaks) because you (Mohammed), you were not there (with the brothers of Joseph), while together they saw fit to set a trap for Joseph. But the majority of men, in spite of your ardent desire (to convince them), will not believe."[24] The reader of the *Bible* will also be distrustful, regarding this alleged revelation, of the intellectual honesty of the Prophet. For the latter [i.e., the Prophet], on the other hand, it cannot be a question of engaging on the terrain of discussion in order to attract the non-believer, the doubter, he who refuses to be humiliated and to prostrate himself. In his eyes [i.e., the Prophet's], such behavior [i.e., the behavior of the non-believer] is nothing other than evil in-itself. Doubting, wanting to understand, demanding proof in order to believe, is to choose the side of *Iblis* [i.e., the Devil]. *Iblis* represents all the doubters, in him all the posers of questions have been

---

[23] Ibid. Surah, 16, 105.
[24] Ibid. Surah, 12, 102-103.

in "*illo tempore*" judged, condemned and chastised. In the same way that *Iblis* is "the Stoned One" because he refused to obey an order from Allah which he considered arbitrary, in like manner all non-believers are doomed to the most frightful tortures: "We have made of Hell a prison for non-believers."[25] Those who want to discuss will be, on the Day of Judgment, hurled into the fires of Hell. On a burning wind and in boiling water, in the shadow of black smoke, they will receive chastisement for their incredulity.[26]

As long and as far as those who hold discussions on good and evil do so for the sake of evil in-itself [i.e., to persecute critical thought] and are dominant in a society, philosophy which is precisely a debate on values and on ultimate norms, will not find a favorable terrain for its development. There is nothing surprising in this, since in the land of Islam, philosophy has succumbed to the hostility of dogmatism and despotism.

3 – The Reality of A Negro-African Philosophy

But what then of the Negro-African world? Is it also hostile to the thought of the absolute? Is there or is there not, a Negro-African philosophy? After having disengaged a specific notion [*une notion déterminée*] of philosophy

---

[25] Ibid. Surah, 17, 8.
[26] Ibid. Surah, 56, 40-43.

rendered more striking in comparison with anti-philosophic cultures, we are conceptually well equipped, we hope, to propose a response to this question. Let us indicate, meanwhile, a supplementary precaution we need to take in order to respond appropriately to the question that has been posed: it is necessary to take into consideration the entire Negro-African world. The pertinence of this observation will become obvious if we notice that the idea that a number of Africans have of Negro-African culture hardly goes beyond the limits of their ethnic group. Thus frequently one hears them attacking the invasion of Western music, intending by that above all, Afro-American and Afro-Cuban music, without suspecting that this music is more African than Western. Keeping things in perspective, one can say that Senghorism has been a victim of a similar myopia in opposing Negro emotion to Greek reason without realizing, as Cheik Anta Diop has shown, that it is the Black peoples of the Nile valley who were, the first, to develop the sciences and techniques and who, according to the *Biblical* formula, "commenced then to become powerful on the land." It would be ill-advised to pretend to take into account the totality of Negro-African culture still so little known. But at least the awareness of its antiquity, of its complexity, of its richness and of its diversity, should make us prudent and distrustful with regard to simplistic generalizations.

From the outset let us take Pharaonic Egypt. Its

thought presents some contrasting traits with the *Bible* and the *Qu'ran* in a manner that seems to us significant. We can only mention them here. A first striking characteristic is the regard for unity, not an immediate unity but one resulting from integration, through a synthesis of all values and not by the exclusion of what presents itself as different. The multiplicity of Egyptian divinities is conceived as forming only one God. Monotheism was nothing but the aborted attempt of Pharaoh Akhenaton. Before and after Akhenaton the Egyptian religion was monotheistic. The reforming Pharaoh wanted only to impose an exclusive monotheism to the detriment of a tradition constituted by an integrative monotheism, a synthesis of all the apparently different Gods. The Egyptian Pantheon is not, as that of the Greeks will later be, constituted by enemy divinities at war with one another. The Egyptian Gods are nothing but different manifestations, the different aspects, of one and the same God. They are like the members of only one body, parts of one and the same whole. The dead do not appear before a solitary God, but before a college of forty-two Gods presided over by a great God [*un grand Dieu*]. He [i.e., the dead person] confesses his innocence to each one with equal respect. Because, fundamentally all these Gods are but one and the same God, and the great God is not a master commanding servants, but a "*primus inter pares.*" They are all the same God, since all are exempt from falsehood and are "nourished" by all that "which is equitable." The preeminence of the supreme God over the other Gods is simply institutional, it does not rest on a superiority of essence.

In a hymn to Amon-Rê, we read:

> Oh the artisan of he-himself whose form nobody knows, perfect appearance which is revealed in a sublime emanation, who fashioned his own images, he created himself.... The Ogdoad was your first manifestation, until you perfected its number, being the One. Your body is hidden among those of the Ancients; you hid yourself as Amon at the head of the gods; you transformed yourself into Tatenen in order to put in the world the primordial divinities at the time of your initial origins... Then you removed yourself, becoming the inhabitant of the sky, established henceforth in the form of the sun. You were the first to come to existence, before anything as of yet existed.[27]

The name of the subject who inaugurates the series of hypostasis is of little importance from a theoretic point of view. The choice of a name is often a question of rivalry between the towns and the Temples. The only thing of importance is the nature of the primitive form under which the God appears. It is either pure indetermination, that is to say matter [i.e., matter without form], or else a being already conscious who makes beings surge-forth by simple verbal utterance. In the first case the perspective is

---

[27] Papyrus 1350 du musée de Leyde (1300-1200 avant notre ére).

materialist, in the second *idealist*. In order to arrive at this conception of a universal Being, a dynamic synthesis of all the Gods, of all beings, a confrontation was evidently required among different Gods, different manifestations of the Absolute, a thinking of the Absolute, in other words a reflection of a philosophic nature. The vocabulary utilized is, of course, generally symbolic and concrete. It is perhaps nothing but a question of translation. In any case, certain texts are formidably abstract. Witness this extract from a dissertation, "The Book of the knowledge of the forms of existence of Rê" dating from some seven or eight centuries before our era:

> When I manifested myself to existence, existence existed. I came into existence in the form of the Existing [*de l'Existant*], which came to existence, for the First Time. Having come to existence in the form of the existence of the Existing, I thus existed. And this is also how existence came to existence, because I am anterior to the Anterior Gods which I made, because I had anteriority over these Anterior Gods, because my name was anterior to theirs, because I made the anterior era just as I made the Anterior Gods. I did all that I desired in this world and I expanded in it...I came thus into existence in the anterior era and a multitude of forms of existence came to existence from this initial beginning, because apparently no form of existence had come to existence in this world. I did all that which I did, being alone, before any other person other than myself was manifest to existence to act in fellowship

with me in these places. I made the modes of existence starting from this force which is in me. I created from Noun (the Indeterminate), being still somnolent and not yet having found any site in which to erect myself. Then my heart proved efficacious, the plan of creation was present in front of me, and I did all that I wanted to do, being alone. I conceived my projects in my heart, and created another mode of existence, and the modes of existence derived from the Existing became a multitude.

I cite this text at length because its philosophic nature cannot be placed in doubt by any philosopher. The effort of reflection, in order to unify the different religions, managed by the Blacks of the Nile valley, millennia before our era, has led to a dynamic conception of the universal being in which the well informed reader cannot fail to recognize the prototype of the Enneads of Plotinus, of the Hegelian Idea, of evolutionism, and also of dialectical materialism.

The second trait which we will mention is even more remarkable. It is the affirmation of the identity between the human being and God. The souls of the deceased in judgment in front of the assembly of the Gods do not cease repeating in the Book of the Dead: I am Osiris, I am Thot, I am Rê, etc...I am pure, I am pure. If the divinity the Gods have, in effect, rests on the fact that "they nourish themselves with that which is equitable," in what way would the just and pure man be different than the Gods? It may seem paradoxical that in a society where the king, the Pharaoh, declared himself God and, as such, had a cult, ordinary men could as easily be identified with the divinity. Perhaps it is precisely because God was not an invisible phantom that the mystery which surrounded him quickly lost its opacity. The process must have thus been the following: the Pharaohs were initially identified with the Gods (which were originally personified natural elements). Then, as a consequence of movements or struggles, of a democratic nature, ordinary men claimed and obtained the generalization of the religious privileges of the Pharaohs: not only the immortality of Ka, but also his divinization [*divinisation*]. Definitively then, the phantom God of anti-philosophical cultures when in question is revealed to human beings in a terrifying and very oppressive manner, unlike the Gods of flesh and bones who cannot indefinitely dissimulate [i.e., hide] their humanity, that is to say their innate equality with the most ordinary human being. The recognition of a fundamental equality among human beings furnishes the basis for philosophic debate, for the thinking of the Absolute, which itself is nothing more than a human possibility.

A last trait of the Egyptian culture that we will point to is very significant for our purpose: the rationality of the supreme code of conduct. To our knowledge (quite limited it is true), neither ethical norms, nor the laws are, in Egypt, delivered-over to a unique Envoy by a God appearing in a great unleashing of elements, of storms, of lightning and of earthquakes. The organization of Egyptian society, the conduct of the Egyptian was meant to be ruled by a central value: the *Maat*. This dense and complex notion designates [i.e., establishes the ground or criteria for] the cosmic, social, and interior [i.e., interior to human life and conduct] order. On the physical level, the *Maat* is exactitude, correct measure; on the social and [political] ethical level, it is truth, justice and order. As one can see, the *Maat* designates an order that is good in-itself but which is incessantly menaced by its contrary, disorder, immoderation, violence. The *Maat* is thus imposed as a duty: for the king, the duty of maintaining or restoring order in social life, justice, [and] the law; for the private individual, the duty of respecting justice and honesty in relation with others or as an effort aimed at controlling the passions in order to acquire self-mastery and goodness. The *Maat* is presented as a fundamental value, and not as a precise and detailed code sent down from the sky in the manner of the Mosaic Law. Nevertheless, it has to be known and applicable to concrete situations. Knowledge of the *Maat* was precisely the focus of the [Egyptian] wisdom writings. The Egyptian sages start from the principle, which will be taken up again thousands of years later by Socrates, that virtue should rest on a science and form the subject of a teaching. These "instructions" [*Les "instructions"*] aim at, as their final result, making the ignorant wise and capable of presenting an exposé of the *Maat*. It is important to note that this teaching is never presented as a divine revelation, but as the fruit of the experience of the ancestors and of the personal reflection of the sage. The author of *The Instruction of Merikaré* concludes his treatise with this formula: "Behold, I have delivered unto you the best of my thoughts. Act according to what is placed before your eyes."

Thus that which, in the *Bible* or the *Qu'ran*, appears as the sin of sins, knowledge, the science of the separation of good and evil, is for the Egyptian an elementary duty. All affirm that virtue is to be the object of a science and of a teaching, the Egyptian sages at the same time also add a safe-guard against [the possibility of] arrogant self-assuredness [hubris] and dogmatism. The *Ptahhotep* counsels:

> Do not be imbued [inflated] with your knowledge
> Consult the ignorant and the learned
> The limits of knowledge are never attained
> None of the learned ever reaches perfection
> The truth is more hidden than a precious stone
> And yet it can be found among humble peasant women.

It is known that it is this mélange of audacity and modesty that led Pythagoras to substitute the word "philosophy" for that of wisdom (s*ophia*). The Egyptians who tended towards the reconciliation of human beings and the Gods instead of their opposition were readily open to the thought that the Gods themselves should seek, consult, and reflect in order to find the truth. As seen in the important text "The Adventures of *Horus* and *Seth*" which shows us the complete Ennead[28] enquiring, consulting, discussing, in order to pronounce [*dire*] the *Maa*t on the conflict opposing the [two] brother Gods. This text can deceive a spirit [i.e., a person] nourished on Christian theological conceptions for which God is "transcendent," that is to say omniscient and omnipotent, he could not stoop-down to the level of seeking and consulting. A spirit [i.e., a person] free of this kind of prejudice will find it, on the contrary, profound and full of interest. The conflict between *Seth* and *Horus* symbolizes the conflict between might and right, between brutality and intelligence, the imprint of humanity, between passions or blind instincts and self-control. The triumph of *Horus* is that of right, of equity, of proper measure and of intelligence, which is to say of order in society, in us and also in the world. The problem of pollution should it not incline us to think that, the ancient African conception according to which social and political disorder engenders disorder in nature, is not and cannot be a pure phantom of the mystical spirit? That which will retain our attention above all else in this allegorical narrative is the method utilized by the Ennead

---

[28] [Etymology: Greek *ennead-*, *enneas*, from *enea* nine + -ad, -as: a group of nine gods; especially: any of several groups of nine gods that were considered to be associated in the mythology and religion of ancient Egypt. *Webster's Third New International Dictionary, Unabridged*. Merriam-Webster, 2002 (http://unabridged.merriam-webster.com)].

for discovering the truth and assuring the triumph of right, of equity, and of intelligence. It is not without effort that it arrives there. The members of the august assembly do not thunder in the clouds amidst the lightning, they proceed to a detailed inquiry, they reason, argue, and even use stratagems, until unanimity is obtained in favor of the *Maat*. The demonstration of the legitimate right of *Horus* will be made on several occasions. It will be repeated until *Seth* himself proclaims it. It is remarkable that Pre-Harakhti, the "Universal Master," the Sun-God, also named, Rê or Atoum, does not dictate his will, he only directs the deliberations of the assembly of the Gods. His personal position will moreover be rejected since he supported *Seth*, contrary to the other Gods, notably *Thot*, guardian of law and equity. One is in fact faced with a collegial direction and not a monarchy. We note the sympathy of Pre-Harakhti for *Seth*, which is to say for brute force. After the defeat of *Seth*, he brings him close to himself: "Let *Seth*, son of *Noun*, be restored to me, so that he can live with me, being close to me as a son: he will shout in the sky and he will be feared."

This work reveals a conception of divinity far removed from the Judeo-Christian conception. That, which constitutes the divinity of a God, is not so much omniscience or omnipotence, but above all respect for the *Maat*, that is to say for truth and for justice. *Seth* himself proved his divinity by finally recognizing the *Maat* and bowing to it, though with much difficulty. As a consequence the human being himself is said to be divine in as much as he searches for and respects the *Maat*. This is why the Egyptian did not hesitate to identify himself with the Gods: I am *Thot*, I am *Osiris*, etc... without letup [*ne cessent*] the souls of the dead proclaim in front of the tribunal of the kingdom of *Osiris*.

Thus if the Egyptian is not content with the devout adoration of the absolute, but makes of it an object of thought, to this extent he is affirmed fundamentally as a philosopher. Everything evidently is not philosophy in the rich Egyptian intellectual production, but only that which is the intrepid thought of the essential, of the absolute. In that which concerns ancient Egypt, the available texts permit the affirmation of the existence of an authentic philosophy which flourished on the banks of the Nile several millenia before Thales, the first pre-Socratic [philosopher]. In this domain, as in so many others, it thus turns out that it was ancient Egypt that opened the way. It pertains to us to proclaim finally that which humanity owes it and that which racist prejudice blocked modern Europeans – contrary to the Ancients – from recognizing.

But what about the rest of Black Africa? Let us skip the Meroitic gymnosophists[29] which the novel of

---

[29] [Gymnosophist, **1**: one of a sect of ancient Hindu philosophers who went naked, lived ascetically, and practiced meditation **2**: one resembling a gymnosophist (*Webster's Third New International Dictionary, Unabridged.* Merriam-Webster, 2002. http://unabridged.merriam-webster.com.]

Héliodore mentions, the Ethiopian [i.e., the Abyssinian[30]] thought studied by Father Claude Sumner, and that which may be produced in Sahelian Africa by the teaching of Greek philosophy in the service [*á la faveur*] of medieval Islam. Let us instead focus on the oral literature that one can actually find today among [Black] Africans living in a traditional milieu. Our attention will especially be focused on the series of tales in which the principal concern seems to be the teaching of stratagems, prudence, and reflection. It is the series of Kulu-the-Turtle, Leuk-the-Hare, and of

---

[30] [*Abyssinian* in contradistinction to *Ethiopian* because, as Claude Sumner explains: "This book [*Classical Ethiopian Philosophy*] on the basic texts of Ethiopian wisdom and thought is primarily concerned with historical Abyssinia and the cultural manifestations of its Semitized inhabitants, not with the peoples and regions now within the political boundaries of present-day Ethiopia. A distinction should therefore be made between 'Abyssinia' and 'Ethiopia.' The former name is derived from the *habäšat* who are well-known from South Arabian and Ethiopic inscriptions; they were colonizers of the West coast of the Red Sea, corresponding nowadays to Northern Ethiopia [and Southern Eritrea], and came from the South-West coast of Arabia, the Yemen. Strictly speaking, the term 'Abyssinia' is only applicable to the region which was the destination of the South Arabian migration. It is thus a term referring to a definite ethnic unit roughly identical with the old Aksumite Empire, while Ethiopian (from *Āιθιoψ*, 'the people with burnt face') is a vague and nondescript term which may justly be applied to the whole country (Semitic, Cushitic, and Nilotic) in its present political boundaries." *Classical Ethiopian Philosophy* (Ethiopia, Addis Ababa: Commercial Printing Press, 1985, page 1). In view of this specification of terms, 'Abyssinian thought' – or better still, 'Habesha thought,' in keeping with the self-designation of the ethnic groups that derive from this history, in both Ethiopia and Eritrea – ought to be the correct term for labeling the material studied by Sumner. That Sumner had to name *Ethiopian* what he knew to be better designated by the term *Abyssinian* has more to do with the expansionist politics of Ethiopian governments, past and present, than with scholarship and learning and will thus not concern us any further.]

Guizo-the-Spider. In these tales we discover a universe lacerated by perpetual conflicts and struggles. They show us also that the human being, to emerge victorious in the struggle of life, has no better weapon or surer guide than his own intelligence. Whatever may be the difficulties, they can always be surmounted thanks to reflection. The heroes of these tales do not follow any "revelation," they do not trust anyone except themselves and their own intelligence. The promotion of human intelligence to the rank of a supreme and unique guide in the struggle of life contrasts violently [i.e., very sharply] with the dominant Semitic traditions which, let us recall, identify such a claim with evil, with sin *par excellence*. From the point of view of Kulu-the-Turtle, or of Leuk-the-Hare, the submission to another, whoever it may be, taken as a guide to existence constitutes, when it concerns an adult, an evident proof of foolishness. He who renounces his own thought in order to blindly follow a guide will sooner or later, on this account, be manipulated by the latter [i.e., his guide] as soon as it is worthwhile for him [i.e., the guide] to do so. This is what is learnt at their own expense by the adversaries, usually much stronger, of Kulu or of Leuk: Ze-the-Panther, or Bouki-the-Hyena. One fine morning Hyena received a visit from an individual calling himself the Son of God. And when the Son of God commands, one executes his will. Hyena submitted with such docility to the will of the Son of God that he himself put himself...in the bag. The Son of God, who was none other than Leuk disguised as a Marabout [a traditional healer and/or "medicine" man], had nothing more to do than to offer him as a present to Fama Korodian.[31] Generally speaking, in the series of sapiential tales [*dans les contes des cycles sapientiaux*], belief in miracles and in the supernatural is presented as the best way [*meilleure façon*] of getting hoodwinked. In a Dagari tale (Borkina-Fassou), Hare advertising his tears, after the death of the monarch, claimed succession to the throne of the dignified king. Astonishment! Not at all troubled, Hare added: "The king is dead, but his soul lives. Let us return to his tomb. I am sure he will testify in my favor." He then [conspired with and] made Squirrel [hiding within the grave] speak, the court was convinced, and Hare became king. Kulu-the-Turtle uses an analogous stratagem to obtain a judgment in his favor in a land dispute which opposed him to Ze-the-Panther. Every portion of land that Kulu wanted to cultivate, Ze claimed as his own. Tired of warring [*De guerre lasse*] Kulu appealed to the judgment of the Ancestors. Two tombs were then excavated. Kulu [conspiring with the Palm-Rat] had a tunnel dug-out by the Palm-Rat, going from his tomb to his house. On the appointed day, he was thrown into his tomb and directly

---

[31] Senegalese tale analyzed by Colardelle-Diarrassouba, *The Hare and the Spider in West African Tales* (10/18, Union Générale des Editions, Paris, pp. 101-104). ["Fama Korodian" I have not been able to find out the meaning or language of these two words, but from the context it is clear that they name a nemesis and/or an antagonist of Bouki-the-Hyena.]

reached his home through the tunnel, while Ze was properly and thoroughly entombed. Kulu [on the other hand] returned to the others with, he claimed, news and gifts from their ancestors! Thus, all the land in litigation was awarded to him.[32] Let us give one last example of the link established, in these sapiential tales, between belief in the supernatural and foolishness. In order to rid himself of an engagement with Kulu-the-Turtle, Ndoe-the-Eagle built himself a nest at the summit of a great Baobab tree and sent Kosso-the-Parrot with this message to Kulu: "Go tell Kulu that I have built my dwelling there where nothing can happen to me." Kulu, upon receiving this message, reflected deeply to find a proper response to the challenge. He prepared some glue, a rope and asked his wife to put it all in a pouch and wrap it up. Kosso took the pouch to Ndoe with the following message from Kulu: "You have built your dwelling there where nothing can ever happen to you: know that, for my part, I have built my dwelling there where nothing will ever get past me." The reply of Kulu is remarkable and highlights the unlimited power that intelligence confers. In fact, Kulu transported by Kosso, will set out to petrify Ndoe. Making casual remarks to his host regarding the scantiness of his progeny he proposes to him a little fertility rite, consisting of coating the wings

---

[32] Stories gathered by Noah Innocent, *The Beti Tales of South-Cameroun*, "The Series of Kulu-the-Turtle and Beme-the-Warthog," Thèse de 3 cycle, Paris, Nanterre, 1973. [No other source or reference specification is given.]

with glue. The rite has one interdiction, one only: "When I have coated your wings with this remedy, said Kulu, do not spread them out. If you spread them out, you will die, and so will all your family." Ndoe and his family conformed to the orders of Kulu, who could thus calmly smear the glue on their wings; and when the glue was quite dry and they were henceforth incapable of making use of their wings, Kulu exterminated them, every last one.[33]

The thought of the authors of these tales is explicit. Credulity, and especially belief in the supernatural, in the magico-religious, constitutes the terrain in which foolishness proliferates. Beme-the-Warthog who, among the Beti [i.e., an ethnic group to be found in the rain forests of Cameroun, Democratic Republic of the Congo, Equatorial Guinea, and Gabon] incarnates stupidity, ignores natural processes and imagines that all that he finds striking and amazing he can actualize by virtue of some supernatural power. He thus has himself skinned alive wishing, "thanks to the supernatural powers bequeathed to him by his father," to imitate Mvomo-the-Boa, who, periodically sheds his skin; another time he breaks his bones attempting, on the force of his magico-religious powers, to "catch" seeds, in flight, like the crows, etc...

While considering Kulu and Leuk as symbols of

---

[33] Ibid. pp. 192-194.

intelligence, our tradition takes great care not to make them perfect beings. They are generally good and just. But sometimes they commit reprehensible acts. In spite of their intelligence, they sometimes show themselves to be foolish. No one is perfect, no one can exhaust wisdom. A tale in the series of Kulu illustrates this quite clearly. One day Kulu filled a big bag full of intelligence and started roaming the world to sell it. He then came upon the enormous trunk of a Baobab tree and settled down waiting for the trunk to rot so that he may continue on his way. Then Mvâga-the-Herpestes[34] happened on him! "What are you doing there, Kulu, my brother," he asked. "I was roaming the world to sell wisdom. Then I found myself in front of this gigantic trunk which is blocking my way. I am neither large enough nor do I have good legs and so I must wait until it rots in order to go on my way." "What," responds Mvâga astonished, "all the time that it will take this trunk to rot, you will stay there getting moldy? A tree has a head and a stem. You go to this side, you arrive at the branches, and if you go to the other, you arrive at the roots." Kulu went to one side, and then to the other, and verified that it was effectively so. Annoyed, he threw away his bag of wisdom and returned home saying to himself: I thought I was the only intelligent one. But no one can

---

[34] A carnivorous mammal similar to a marten, says Th. Tsala in his Ewondo dictionary [The term "marten" names any of the small carnivorous mammals, like the weasel but larger, that live in trees and have a long slender body].

know how to exhaust wisdom.[35] Thus no one has a monopoly of perfection and of intelligence, no one, not even God himself. The traditional African thinker does not only distrust the son of God and miracle workers,[36] but equally God himself whom he does not hesitate to take on. Spider, for example, declares:

> God, God, but one can fool him
> All it takes is guts
> God, God, but one can fool him
> He is so old that he does not see a thing.[37]

In another tale related by Colardelle-Diarrassouba we see Spider grappling with God during an assembly. God claims that a knife cut is more harmful than slander. Spider maintains the opposite view: "Hey, grand-father-God, it is true that a knife cut hurts, but not as much as slander." The ethical discussion is prolonged without conclusion, and they abandon it. Then one night, Spider does something wicked under the tree of the Good Lord. On the morrow when the sacrilege is discovered the assembly is convened to seek out the culprit. Spider contrives to convince the assembly that the guilty party is none other than God himself. Ashamed, he [i.e., God]

---

[35] This tale is from my village, Endama [Cameroun].

[36] We have mentioned in this regard the series of Bembe. See also the tale *Lies and Truth*. [No other source or reference specification is given.]

[37] Cf. B. Dadié, *Pagne noir*, p. 64 Présence Africaine. [No other source or reference specification is given.]

departs to the bushes, knife in hand, to kill himself. At which point Spider sends after him before the fatal did is done and declares to the assembly: "It is I who did the deed, it was not he; I acted in this way to prove that slander does more harm than a knife cut."[38] Spider thus convicted God of error. As Colardelle-Diarrassouba has observed, God is omnipresent in the series of the Spider. The latter is bent on pitting himself against God and often it is God who gets the worst of it. Noah Innocent also reports a tale in which Kulu succeeds in fooling God in order to get out of an imprudent agreement that he had made so as to wed one of God's daughters. He had promised to be buried with his father-in-law if ever he [i.e., the father-in-law] died before him. Soon, thereafter, this indeed happened. But Kulu found a stratagem to escape from death.[39] Let us note in passing that God, according to these tales, has a family, he dies just like a human being. This is not the Semitic God, solitary and a-temporal, but the primordial ancestor.

From our exposé an idea has been disengaged [*dégage*] that is so atypical of the usual way of understanding traditional African thought that one has to question the real significance of the cited texts. For if it is true, as Noah and Colardelle-Diarrassouba think that Kulu and Leuk are initiates [of this traditional thought], one will have to

---

[38] Colardelle-Diarrassouba, op. cit. pp. 268-269.
[39] Noah Innocent, op. cit., p. 156.

admit that the series of tales in which they are the heroes express and veil, at the same time, through the mediation of an animalist [*animalier*] and comic symbolism, the most profound of traditional thought. This traditional thought can [thus] be defined as being essentially the exhaltation of intelligence in the service of right, the refusal to make it the monopoly of a unique being and the recognition of the fact that wisdom is available [*á la disposition de*] to all those who make an effort [*prennent la peine*] to acquire it.

1. Traditional African thought places *nothing above intelligence*. And this [i.e., intelligence] is recognized as the faculty of inventing solutions to all possible problems on the basis of knowledge of and respect for objective processes, of basing conduct on what one *judges* to be good or bad, foolishness consists in unloading this responsibility onto others, of putting *faith* on their judgment, of letting oneself be dictated to, without understanding, the values and rules of conduct. This is a finding that is far from being banal if one considers that in Semitic cultures the dominant tradition reverses these positions by identifying the adjudication of good and bad, the thinking of values, with evil in-itself, and makes of "faith," that is to say credulity, the condition of salvation.

2. Profound African thought *refuses* to recognize in anyone *the monopoly of intelligence and ethical* *perfection*. All real beings – or beings considered as such – humans or Gods, are intellectually limited and morally imperfect. No one is shielded from error or fault. As a consequence, no one, human or God, has grounds to arrogate to himself the right of thinking and judging for the entire world and of dictating to all the truth and the norms of conduct. The limitation of all real beings [or beings considered as such] is the condition for the exchange of ideas, of openness. As soon as the omniscience and the perfection of a real being is posited, simultaneously and in principle dogmatism and enclosure are also posited, since the alleged omniscience and perfection are invoked only in order to justify socio-political absolutism, effective or potential. And so the struggle against metaphysical dogmatism which gives meaning to traditional thought gets entangled with the struggle against political absolutism and the arbitrariness of power. The absolute, values and ultimate norms, fundamental truths, are not the will and the ideas of a perfect unique being, but the results of a collective effort, of research and reflection undertaken in common, the existence of a perfect unique being is thus an inadmissible point. In this way traditional African thought avoids in principle the possibility of revelation, of a proclamation of the truth, of values and of norms made once and for all, that would exempt us from researching and defining them for ourselves. Kulu, Leuk, contest all forms of absolutism. Traditional African thought has such fear of absolutism that it takes care [*qu'elle prend soin*] to underline the limits in the intelligence and moral value of even the champions themselves of intelligence and of rights.

If it is true that it [i.e., traditional African thought] posits the limitation and imperfection of all real beings or those considered as such, [then] traditional African thought posits in principle the necessity for an effort, for a reflection in common, for an exchange of views, for a debate to determine the ultimate values and norms, it is thus also true by the same token that it is authentically philosophic, because we had defined philosophy as the debate on the essential, on the absolute. This is a debate in principle open to all owing to the limitation of those who participate, that is to say by right, to all adult human beings, because wisdom is, by right, accessible to all.

This wisdom more precious than gold and which allows each one to situate himself in the world and to lead his boat to a good port at whatever time, Spider tried to keep all for himself by enclosing it in a hermetically sealed jar. He was calmly on his way with his son Eban until he found the way blocked by a tree. Spider, not being able to go around the obstacle, set his jar on top of it. But the jar slid, fell, it broke and wisdom spread out, carried by the wind. That is to say each human being obtained a little-bit of this wisdom.[40]

---

[40] Texte de B. Dadié, cite par Colardelle-Diarrassouba op., cit., pp. 175 – 176.

In comparing actual African traditional thought expressed in these philosophical tales to the thought of ancient Egypt, it is easy to find, besides the evident differences, similarities that are no less evident. In both cases, intelligence and right oppose brutal force and injustice; in both cases, intelligence and right triumph over brutality and injustice. The opposition of Kulu-the-Turtle to Ze-the-Panther or Bembe-the-Warthog, or for that matter of Leuk-the-Hare to Bouki-the-Hyena, reproduces in essence the conflict between Horus, weak but intelligent, and Seth strong, unjust, and un-reflective. In both cases the intelligent personality is characterized not only by circumspection but equally by moderation and self-mastery, and his adversary by credulity, naïveté, and servitude [*l'asservissement*] to brutal passions. The hero of thought, of good judgment and of right has recourse, in both cases to the same arms, for confounding foolishness and injustice. He moves forth less by abstract argumentation than by ruse [i.e., stratagems]. It is a question of putting the adversary in a situation in which he will recognize and proclaim for the sake of interest that which he refused to admit for the sake of interest. Seth, because he is the stronger, intends to inherit the crown of Osiris by asserting his force. Chou intervenes before Atoum: "Justice comes before force, realize this in giving the function to Horus." Thot supports the proposition: "It is just, a million times." As Seth, blinded by his ambition, refuses to accept reason, Isis appears to him in the form of a beautiful woman. Seth, moved by a violent desire, wants to possess her. Isis places a condition: that Seth undertake the defense of a son, whom a stranger wants to defraud, by force, of the herd left by his father. Seth responds indignantly: "Is one going to give the livestock to a stranger while the son of the father of the family is still alive?"

Isis, throwing off her disguise, addresses Seth in these terms: "Weep for yourself: it is your own mouth which has pronounced it, your own intelligence has judged you, yourself. What more do you want?"[41] An analogous stratagem is utilized in "Truth and Lie," a philosophic tale from the *New Kingdom*. Truth had misplaced or damaged a knife that his brother Lie had lent him. The case is brought before the Gods. Lie accuses his brother of theft and refuses to accept any reparations by attributing, to his knife, extraordinary qualities. Truth is condemned to have his eyes gouged and to become his brother's door-man. Much later, the son of Truth accuses, in the presence of the Gods, his uncle Lie of having led astray an ox of extraordinary size: "This cannot be true, reply the Gods, for we have never seen an ox of such size." To which, the boy retorts: "And does there exist such an extraordinary knife (as claimed at the earlier hearing)?" We see breaking through here, let it be said in passing, a critique of the marvelous, of belief in the extraordinary. This process of

---

[41] Op., cit., p. 67.

refutation, classic among the Egyptians, is currently found in the philosophic tales of the oral literature of the rest of Black Africa. Let us give a single example. Ze-the-Panther was claiming from Nkoa-the-Antelope the lambs of a ram from among the herd of the latter. Kulu-the-Turtle arrived late to the assembly of the animals convened to examine the dispute. Questioned by Ze for the reasons of his tardiness, Kulu answered that he had been a witness to a strange event: "a male antelope was having labor pains; during this time I did my utmost to assist him." And Ze cried out against the lie: "Where have you ever seen a male in labor?" – "Ze, my brother" continued Kulu "you yourself have pronounced your own condemnation; you said that you placed in the herd of Nkoa a ram, that is to say, a male animal: Does a ram have young?" Asked Kulu, whereupon the gathered animals dispersed. Ze, furious, seized Kulu with the intention of smashing him against a rock. Kulu mocked Ze by making him believe that he was a rock and that rocks could not do him any harm, one could kill him only by throwing him in a swamp. Right away the foolish beast executed the suggestion. Thus, Kulu sank in the mud and got away.[42]

The resemblance in the content of this tale and of that of "Truth and Lie" does not need to be highlighted [it is obvious]: the same ability to make the liar contradict himself, the same critique of belief in the miraculous. The

---

[42] Noah Innocent, op., cit., pp. 219 – 221.

process rests on a completely anthropological conception: he in whom opinions are dictated by passions is not susceptible, and/or responsive, to purely abstract argumentations. To change his opinions one has to change, and it suffices to change, the direction of his desires. Superstition, belief in miracles, in supernaturalism, rests essentially on the tyrannical hold that desire and passion have over the greater part of humanity. This is what is shown [*montré*] by a Malinke tale, "Lie and Truth" published by Blaise Cendrars in his *Anthologie Nègre*. The title is identical to that of the Egyptian tale mentioned above. But the Malinke tale no longer wants to underline the final triumph of Truth, but the immense empire of Lies that rules over the majority of humankind. Lie and Truth were traveling together. Truth speaking sincerely hurt the sentiments of their hosts who, thus infuriated, threw him out. Lie, on the contrary, while lavishing remarks that always went along with the desires and wishes of their hosts, went so far as to affirm that he had the power to raise the dead. By such means, he had himself welcomed in a princely fashion and obtained all that he needed without evidently resurrecting anyone.[43]

Let us observe finally that the thinker of traditional Black Africa and the Egyptian thinker are in accord in refusing omniscience and ethical perfection to any being whatsoever and admit that all human beings are capable,

---

[43] Blaise Cendrars, *Anthologie Nègre*, Buchet/Chastel, pp. 145 – 148. [No other source or reference specification is given.]

more or less [*plus ou moins*], of acquiring them [i.e., knowledge and ethics]. In this way, they avoid the idea of revelation, of any truth proclaimed once and for all and posit the necessity for reflection, for research, and for the exchange of ideas as the only way of accessing the truth [of whatever is in question on any particular occasion]. And this need to debate the essential, as we know is another name for the philosophic need. These elements of resemblance between Egyptian thought and the thought of the rest of Black Africa seem to us sufficiently numerous and important to authorize the affirmation of the existence of a profound African philosophic tradition going back to its most remote antiquity.

III. THE PROBLEMS OF AN AFRICAN PHILOSOPHY OF AND FOR OUR TIME:

In starting from European texts and from the European word "philosophy," in order to disengage [and secure] the notion of philosophy [*la notion de philosophie*], we have taken care to indicate that the choice of this starting point does not implicate us in any judgment of value on European philosophy, it does not signify either adoption or rejection of philosophy in the European sense of the term. After having demonstrated the existence of philosophy in the traditional African culture, we should also, and more energetically, specify that this recognition does not make us, *ipso facto*, an adept [*un adepte*] of the African philosophy whose reality we have demonstrated. The exploration of the past, the examination of our traditional cultures obeys a concern for objectivity and for self-knowledge. It is important for us to know ourselves such as we are, as the past, recent or remote, has formed us, to truly apprehend the achievement of our ancestors, in all of its diversity. It should neither be impoverished nor disfigured. But some biased "researchers" have affirmed with suspect facility and insistence the essential and incurable religious character of the Negro with the, hardly veiled, intention of immunizing him against modern ideologies, notably "atheistic" Marxism. One must react against such a tendency which leads to obscuring aspects of our cultural traditions that contradict the religious prejudice and the theory of anchoring stones [*pierres d'attente*].

But, the question of knowing what philosophy to adopt or even if it is necessary to philosophize is not resolved [or answered] in this way. Thus is posed, relative to philosophy, a general and a specific question.

1. *The general question* of knowing whether one should or should not opt for philosophy is the same as asking if we should take thought as the supreme guide of life or if it is to another instance of life that this role is to be assigned. By thought, we mean, let us remember, the power of examining and of confronting diverse representations, doctrines, ideologies, in order to retain those which we judge most in conformity with the truth, that is to say, to that which is, can, or should be. Thought understood in this way opposes all spontaneous fidelity, without critical examination, to any conception or doctrine whatsoever, under the pretext that it is purveyed by a superior being: God, ancestor, jinni, seer, etc... As far as we are concerned, we hold thought to be that which is the most elevated manifestation in the known world [*dans le monde connu*]. We maintain in effect that of all known beings, the human being is the only one that thinks, and for this reason, prevails over all. We maintain further that among human beings those, individuals or peoples, who develop the universal faculty of thinking, will prevail in the long run over those who stifle or neglect it. To admit that thought is that which is the most elevated manifestation in the world, is to admit also that it should never be directed and that it is rather to it that the right reverts of directing the life of the beings in whom it is manifested. As to thoughtlessness, it is not an option. Humanity cannot permit itself to imitate the lilies of the fields and the birds of the sky that neither sow nor reap, for, apparently, no one will render it this service. If humans neglect sowing and reaping, thinking and caring for the conditions of their lives, they will most certainly perish.

On another plane, thought furnishes a solid base for autonomy and equality. All limitation of thought leads to a limitation of equality or results in it. Thought is a universal human faculty whose exercise engages everyone personally. That which is named, in mythological systems, faith or belief authorizes on the contrary a fundamentally asymmetrical structure that exudes dependence, because it is always about submitting to a superior being in that which concerns [questions of] truth and the norms of comportment [or societal behavior]. Such systems are grounded on the old myth of humanity-as-the-flock-of-God. It is incumbent on the shepherd to think and to decide and on the sheep to follow that which the shepherd thinks and decides. Little does it matter that he decides to conduct them to pasture or to the slaughter house, for the sheep will follow with equal docility. In like manner God, in his omniscience and in his goodness reveals to human beings his thoughts and his will to which they must submit with a totally sheepish docility. Between God who revels and the human being who believes in the revelation is established an inequality in essence analogous to that which exists between the shepherd and the sheep. The sheep at least see their shepherd and recognize his voice. The human flock is not that privileged. The Divine Shepherd does not show himself to his flock, and it pleases him, it seems, to resort to intermediaries, to be sure we only hear the voices of other humans who are said to be his envoys or his representatives. Under these conditions, how do we know if it is he who speaks to us, to us his flock, and not the wolf, how do we know if he even speaks and if we really have a shepherd? With thought [i.e., philosophy], on the other hand we are on the firm ground of direct [*intime*] experience, because the exercise of thought is an activity which is essentially ours and is essentially conscious. It is the foundation of autonomy, because it is personal in essence, it is also the foundation of equality because it is a universal human faculty.

Opting for philosophy has then the significance of a commitment to autonomy and equality. Negatively it signifies the refusal of the miraculous, of all the mythologies and all the ideologies that invite us, directly or indirectly, explicitly or implicitly, to renounce our power of examining and judging for ourselves and confer this responsibility on an other; consequently, all those who, in the name of God, of History, of Civilization, of positivity [*positivité*], come to denigrate thought or attempt to reduce its significance will be asked, by us, to step aside and allow us to interrogate [or examine], without an intermediary, natural or socio-historical reality, as well as God himself. It is necessary to add that in elevating thought to the supreme position of guiding our conduct, we do not fail to recognize the reality and importance of *the heart* and of the *imagination*. We only affirm that passions [i.e., the heart] just as any other imaginary representation must be examined, controlled and judged, otherwise we would hardly be aware of having fallen, as instruments, into the hands of a crafty-evil genius a past master in the art of manipulating the credulity and naïveté of the masses.

Philosophy, that is to say the thought of the essential, thus grounds liberty and equality, but this determination is not unilateral. The thought of the essential, on its part, cannot be instituted, take root, and blossom without a socio-political milieu favorable to discussion. Pure brutality, for example, excludes all debate. Philosophic thought is not pure, it is not self-sufficient and it cannot thus experience an autonomous development which is independent of an institutional and sociological context. Thought spreads-out [*déploie*] abundantly [*largement*] when the socio-political milieu encourages it, when it solicits it. In itself [*En elle-même*], the thought of the essential [i.e., philosophy] is inscribed in the process of creation that opens-on-to [*qui débouche*] concrete praxis, it is an aspect, a moment, a phase: the theoretic phase [of concrete praxis]. Because, originally, thought was but an aspect of the global process of the creation and transformation of the given [*du donné*], there exists between it and [political] power a profound relation. It is through thought in effect that the human being elevates himself above the given, it is through it [i.e., thought] that he gives himself other possibilities, that he compares them, confronts them, that he fore-sees [*pré-voit*] the process through which each of these possibilities could or could not be realized. This power of fore-sight [*pré-vision*] and of pre-elaboration [*pré-élaboration*] limits considerably fumbling and errors and is translated into an increase of power which makes of the human being the most powerful being in the *known* world [*monde connu*]. Knowledge is thus the source of power. Power over the elements is sustained by knowledge of the elements, and power over human beings, spiritual [i.e., cultural] power is sustained by knowledge of human beings, of their heart and of their spirit [i.e., culture]. But to say that the power of transforming, of creating, constitutes the principal result of knowledge is to recognize that power is the crowning and ultimate end-result of knowledge. It is not for the mere pleasure of contemplating the world that the human being seeks to know the real, but with the aim of transforming it, of controlling it in order to adapt it [*l'adapter*] to his needs and to his aspirations or to transform himself so as to adapt himself to it. There is no longer art for art's sake, nor pure knowledge, knowledge for its own sake. Knowledge must augment our control over reality and improve our condition in the world.

In a living culture [*Dans une culture vivante*], thought is held-captive [*retenue*] by the questions that present a concrete interest for life. And because the profound source of knowledge is practice, theoretic activity cannot long maintain itself if it is cut-off from all power and from any possibility of concretization [*concrétisation*]. Without power, knowledge appears to be object-less [*sans objet*] and vain [i.e., purposeless], like something external to the seriousness of life. That which is foreign [*étranger*] to the processes of practical life ceases being a real concern and sooner or later disappears from the horizon of thought.

Living knowledge [*Le savoir vivant*] ends by limiting itself to the sphere of real preoccupations. Greek philosophic thought culminated in the affirmation of the power of Athens. Modern European philosophy has been, essentially, the work of England, France and above all Germany. Why, if not because these countries have also been the principal European and world powers for the last three centuries. Because they were world powers, these countries felt responsible for the destiny of the world. It is natural that their thought took the same dimensions as their concrete concerns, that is to say universal dimensions. Powerful peoples or those who aspire to become so have concerns proportionate to their responsibilities or to their ambitions. The peoples who are weak and without ambitions have, likewise, preoccupations limited to their field of activity. A small country has the feeling that the fate of the world hardly ever depends on it, but on the great powers. It would therefore have the tendency to limit its thinking to its real concerns, which are bound to be narrow. What good is it in effect to think about the world, [and] of its destiny if we can do nothing to modify and ameliorate it? The feeling of powerlessness produces indifference in regard to that over which we have no control. Why did Greece, which gave the world Democracy, Plato, and Aristotle, itself became philosophically sterile, if not because it no longer felt responsible for the course of the world, it had lost power and with it its self-confidence and its historical assuredness? And the day, perhaps less distant than it seems, when England, France, and Germany lose their responsibilities as world powers, this day will also mark the decline of their philosophic flourishing [*essor philosophique*]. It is true that the feeling of power or powerlessness [*d'impuissance*] is subjective, and an objectively very feeble people can show great historic assurance and audacity of thought if it ignores its real powerlessness and the existence of more important peoples capable of paralyzing it. These remarks lead us to think that the possibility of a philosophical renaissance in Africa is tied to its political and economic destiny. Africa will not be able to formulate a great contemporary philosophy unless it becomes or tends to become, without provoking a smile [*sans prêter à sourire*], a great contemporary power capable of declaring itself responsible for the lot of the world. It is this ambition which, without a doubt, furnishes the necessary energy to contemporary African philosophic efforts. The élan that sustains them [i.e., African philosophic efforts] would certainly relapse [*retomberait*] with the loss of such a hope, since it is true that knowledge hardly-ever ventures far beyond our effective preoccupations and ambitions.

Power, or perhaps more accurately, the consciousness of power, seems thus to be a necessary condition for philosophy, but not a sufficient one. For, power can be organized on an absolutist and despotic foundation intolerant [*ne tolerant*] of any debate on its founding principles. In such a case, it is myth that predominates and not philosophy. Philosophy cannot prosper under despotism other than by combating and refuting it.

2. *To the general question*: for or against philosophy? We have firmly pronounced ourselves in favor of philosophy. Moving on to *the specific question*: which philosophy for Africa? We will answer succinctly: a philosophy which will articulate a critique [*une philosophie qui soit la saisie critique*], the theory of that which is, of that which we are and will become, in the center of that which is or is on the way of becoming [*au sein de ce qui est ou est en cours*], of that which we want, the forethought/foresight [*prevision*] of the conditions for the actualization [*réalissation*] of our fundamental design, of the principal obstacles that impede us and of the manner of surmounting them.[44]

a. *Our Present Condition*
Actually, Africa is, as a whole, under the control of a world-wide system of domination and of exploitation. International capitalism imposed itself on our societies thanks to its superior physical force which it derived from scientific knowledge of the elements and of natural processes, and the application of this knowledge to military and productive activity. On the other hand,

---

[44] [In other words, for Towa, these are the concrete theoretic tasks of and for a contemporary African philosophy which he will now briefly outline in six interconnected points (a – f).]

slavers, colonialists and neocolonialists have always found in all indigenous societies accomplices, leaders or popular figures [*hommes du people*], ready to collaborate with them in return for immediate personal gain. This alliance, on the social and political level, with morally unhealthy forces, has been prolonged, in the cultural domain, by the encouragement of all the elements that, in the traditional society, were judged to be favorable to the reinforcement of domination. Capitalist and imperialist Europe combated, in the invaded societies, all the forces – i.e., human beings, institutions, beliefs, customs – hostile to slavery, that is to say all that which was most wholesome in these societies. With a vengeance [*En revanche*], writes Césaire, it

> [Europe] made a firm alliance with all the indigenous feudalists who agreed to serve; it devised with them obscene plots; rendered their tyranny more effective and efficient, and its actions have tended towards nothing less than the artificially prolonged survival of the most pernicious aspects of the local past. Colonialist Europe grafted modern abuse on to ancient inequality.[45]

Ideologically, the effort of imperialism consists in

---

[45] Aimé Césaire, *Discours sur le Colonialisme* (Paris, France: Presence Africaine, 1955), p. 22. [Discourse on Colonialism (New York: Monthly Review Press, 1972), p. 24. Towa's rendition of the quote varies slightly from that found in the cited text, and in the Standard English translation, and he also gives pages 25-26 as the location for the quoted passage.]

preventing the colonized from achieving self-awareness [*prise de conscience*] of their real condition of being dominated and exploited, [this it does] by deprecating the colonized in their own eyes and presenting [to them] the new course imprinted on their history [by colonialism] as beneficial to them. Such that, the colonized themselves end by accepting their new condition and collaborating in their own exploitation. It is not enough for imperialism to have slaves, it is also necessary that they be content with their lot.

The colonized, like all enslaved human beings, is a deposed [*déchu*][46] being in the strong sense of the word. A dominated human being is by definition essentially passive. It is forbidden to him to express his needs and his aspirations, to conceive his future and to decide on it. He is inserted, as an instrument [*á titre d'instrument*], in the creative praxis of the master. This amounts to saying that he has lost the historic initiative, the right to undertake and to create. The thinking [*pensée*] of the enslaved human being (who has not yet revolted) slumbers, his will is dulled: due to a lack of exercise. As a result of the phenomenon of overcompensation, well known to psychoanalysis, his biological-instinctive functions

---

[46] [The enslaved human being is "deposed" of his humanity, just as a king when "deposed," or dethroned, is denied the right to his throne, that which makes him a king. In like manner, in being enslaved, the enslaved, is denied or "deposed" of his/her humanity, of that which makes him/her human i.e., the lived actuality and power of making decisions, i.e., self-determination.]

develop abnormally. The *atrophy* of thought [i.e., of reason] and of the will, which are the highest powers of properly human conscious creativity, are coupled with a *hypertrophy* of emotivism [*l'émotivité*], of instinctual and of magico-religious comportment.[47] This lowered-status [*déchéance*] of the dominated human being is then invoked to explain and justify domination, which in truth [*qu'en réalité*], is itself the end result [of this domination]. Enslavement naturalizes, animalizes the human being. This is a crime against humanity and should be considered as absolute evil.

b. *Our Goal*
These remarks reveal the profound meaning of the anti-colonialist movement. A people that struggles for its liberation undertakes to reconquer its lost humanity, that is to say, the power to express itself and to conceive, to decide and to actualize that which it has decided upon. As regards our continent, the struggle for liberation envisions or should envision the emergence of a prosperous and

---

[47] The magico-religious comportment is motivated by the impatience of desire which does not fulfill itself through the mediation of thought and work and, in this manner, moves the human being closer to the animal, dominated by desire and instinct and incapable of thought and of work properly speaking. [This is so even if] it is true that the magico-religious comportment presupposes a power of the imagination of which no animal is capable and which manifests itself in the fantastic objectification of the objects of desire, of fear, and of affectivity in general by recourse to a complex symbolism.

powerful Africa, centered-on-itself [*auto-centrée*], an autonomous Africa with its own center of needs and aspirations, of expression, of conception, of decision and of actualization [*réalisation*] on the political, economic, and cultural level. Such is the meaning of the revolution that is to be brought about [*qu'il s'agit d'opérer*]. Imperialism will spare no effort to prevent it and we should not spare ourselves any sacrifice in order to realize it [*pour l'imposer*].

It is important to be conscious of the real dimensions of the enterprise and to identify exactly the enemy to be smashed [*abattre*]. The enemy, is not only the foreign invader, but equally, in our societies, all the forces (human beings, institutions, social structures, customs, beliefs) that have been and still are its accomplices, all the gaps [*lacunes*] that facilitated its [i.e., the foreign invaders] enterprise. In these conditions, to make the revolution no longer means only to rid ourselves of the foreigner, but equally to be deeply transformed: the revolution has to be at the same time a self-revolution [*auto-révolution*]. The global system of domination and of exploitation is not constituted uniquely [*uniquement*] by the forces of the center; it finds support in the very heart [*au sein meme*] of enslaved populations and cultures. It cannot therefore be broken without a social and cultural revolution through which its local support is stamped-out.

Fierce struggle against the internal forces of the global system of domination and of oppression, but also solidarity with all the forces which, the world over, are combating the monster. To the global system of oppression and of exploitation, the revolutionary forces must oppose an anti-imperialist front which is also global.

c. *Domesticating Science and Technology*
Finally, we must come to understand that the power of the international bourgeoisie is ultimately the power of matter domesticated by science and technology. If we also want to be strong – and it is indeed necessary if we are resolved to free ourselves from European [i.e., Western] imperialism – it is easy to see what we have to do: master in our turn modern science and technology in order to have at our disposal the forces of matter, [and yet] instead of appropriating the materialism of industrial civilization we hide behind the pretext that the Negro is essentially religious and spiritual. Was this the spirituality that drove the "negro kings" to sell their brothers to slavers for a little brandy or some measure of cloth? And the millions of African soldiers, who, across the continent, helped and still help the colonialist and the racists in massacring their own [people], is this for love of the spirit? And neocolonialism itself does it not essentially rest on corruption and our limitless avidity for the products of this materialist civilization so half heartedly criticized? In fact, what do they think of us those who have put in place [i.e., instituted] neocolonialism? A banker explains to his colleagues frightened [*effrayés*] by the idea of

independence:

> Chin up, gentlemen. Chin up, I say. You've got to wed the spirit of the times. I don't say love her, it's enough to wed her. There's nothing so frightening about this independence....
>
> No credit due. It's normal after twenty years in the tropics, time to find out plenty. To handle savages, there are two ways: One is the club, but that's seen better days. The other is the purse....
>
> What do their leaders want? They want to be Presidents, ministers, living in luxury. In short, the purse! High-powered cars, Villas, high wages, cushy bank accounts. Spare no expense. Just grease their palms and stuff them. The investment will pay off. You'll see, their hearts will melt. And presently those smirking, smiling politicians will be a special class between us and their people. They'll hold the people down provided we tie them with bonds—well, maybe not of friendship, that's out of date in this century— But knots and tangles of complicity.[48]

This text gives us an unflattering image of ourselves, whose veracity cannot be totally denied. As always, the system that they have established functions. Thus, in what could the anti-materialism of those who are ready to sacrifice all for material gain, including their conscience and soul, consist of? Instead of sinking into corruption in

---

[48] Aimé Césaire, *Une Saison au Congo* (Ed., du Seuil, 1966), pp. 19 – 21. [*A Season in the Congo*, trans., Ralph Manheim (New York: Grove Press, 1968), pp. 11 – 13. The quotation is from Scene 4. It is a selection from the remarks of the Fifth Banker].

order to acquire industrial products, instead of demanding from industrial powers technical assistance, arms and military instructors in order to massacre our famished people...one could well think that it would be more spiritual to become technicians ourselves so as to produce in abundance the material goods which we cannot do without.

It seems that [*Il semble bien que*] the verbal opposition to materialism, in the name of God and the spirit, rests on a misunderstanding concerning the nature of spirit. It is through knowledge of natural phenomena and the control that he exercises over them, that God, for example, in *Genesis*, psalm 104 in the book of Job, establishes his transcendence, his absolute superiority over the human being. God, that is according to the theologians, the Absolute Spirit, is such because he knows and governs the world; and the human being, in *Biblical* texts, must submit to God by reason of his ignorance of the universe and his powerlessness in front of the unleashed elements and natural beings. God does not despise [*dédaigne*] presenting himself as an engineer who, to impose limits on the sea, installed bolts and swing-doors, who has drawn a line on the earth, and who has set the earth on a base that he has constructed, etc...[49] But see how the human being, by his own efforts, has developed knowledge and means of action, limited to be sure, but less illusory than those that

---

[49] *Job*, 38, 4 – 11.

Yahweh displays in the *Bible*. In one blow science and power cease, according to our theologians, being the attributes of the Spirit [i.e., God] to become nothing more than the manifestations of the materialism of modern civilization! If knowledge and control of phenomena no longer define the Spirit [i.e., God] it will hence forth be known as pure consciousness, a pure insubstantial interiority without consistency.

The verbal denigration of science and of modern technology cannot, in our opinion, seriously affect their prestige and their control over us. The human being is in effect a natural being, composed of material elements. Therefore, he who has dominion over the elements and natural phenomena equally has dominion over him. The human being has need of the elements to sustain his material substance; he fears disintegration by privation or by aggression. To secure control of the elements and of other natural phenomena through science and technology is then to have secured the right of life and death over those who ignore this secret of power. Inequality in this domain is ineluctably [*inéluctablement*] translated into inequality on the political domain. Those who are superior in the field of knowledge and the control of natural phenomena establish their dominion over the others. One must understand that science and modern technology furnish the means of domination or of liberation that are altogether much more reliable than the so-called supernatural powers of the personages of *Biblical* mythology which are nothing more than the phantoms of the magico-religious mentality of the Hebrews.

A reasonable conception of spirit would not, in our opinion, exclude science and power from the phenomena that it establishes. Because, from what we know of it, spirit is above all, power of representation, of signification, of thought, and of choice. Representations, thoughts, decisions, constitute so many aspects, so many phases of rational praxis, [and] of the transformation of reality. In sum, spirit is activity. To act means to clash [*heurter*] with the resistance of the given objective world and defeat [*vaincre*] this resistance in transforming the established reality by making it conform to our needs and to our subjective conceptions. In other words, it is in the world and on the objective world that spirit is affirmed and deployed; spirit, that is to say, human beings, beings of flesh and bones who experience needs, who conceive, discuss their conceptions and act in accordance with the resulting ideas. If such is spirit, then a civilization that cultivates reflection and action founded on thought cannot be a total stranger to it. Those who proclaim themselves partisans of the spirit and at the same time stand against the science and technology of industrial civilization seem not to have understood that which spirit really is. To be opposed to thought and to rational praxis, to action based on thought, is surely to be opposed to spirit. One sees from this that the enemies of spirit are not the ones that are believed to be so. If it is true, for example, that having faith, is to renounce thinking the content of faith [i.e., critically and rationally reflecting on what we are asked to believe], that is to say, the essential, one must then admit that this is a mutilation of thought and thus of spirit. The formation of representations is certainly an activity of spirit, but the critical examination of representations in order to verify their objectivity rises [*relève*] to a form of spirit which is much more superior to spontaneous and naïve belief, the adherence [*l'adhésion*] without examination to incomprehensible representations. Those who elevate themselves to the thinking [i.e., critical questioning] of representations and of beliefs are consequently better positioned [*plus fondés*] to claim spirit as their own than those who stop at simple representations forbidding themselves all questioning of incomprehensible beliefs, that is to say, in plain language, absurdities. The novel by Cheikh Hamidou Kane, *Ambiguous Adventure* (1961), is entirely based on the opposition between industrial civilization which is [taken as] nothing more than the proliferation of appearances and the civilization of the Diallobe, symbol of the civilizations of the Third World based, according to the author, on the belief in God, the Absolute Spirit. Now throughout the book, Kane stirs-up [*agite*] diverse questions: the problem of work, of wealth, of life, of the diversity of cultures, etc...and their relation to God. But on God himself no real question is posed, no discussion engaged. He tells us that the human being "is born in a forest of questions."[50] But a closer look reveals, however, that these are not real questions that call for a debate. By questions the author means, on the one hand, the most elementary and necessary needs of the [human] organism, and on the other, the aspirations of the heart. The famished stomach does not pose questions: it dictates. It is the same with tired limbs: "I must eat, feed me," orders the stomach. "Are we finally going to rest? Let us, could we?" murmur the limbs. To the stomach and to the limbs, the human being gives the appropriate response, and is happy. "I am alone, I am afraid of being alone...find someone to love me," implores a voice. "I am afraid, I am afraid. What is my country of origin? Who brought me here? Where are they taking me?" asks this particularly plaintive voice, which laments day and night. The human being rises and goes in search of other human beings. Then, he gets up to pray.[51] The spontaneity and the immediacy of the reactions are striking. The intention of the author is to indicate to us that the metaphysical question, the need for God, is as natural and vital a need as the need for food and rest, and that it calls for an equally

---

[50] Cheikh Hamidou Kane, *L'aventure ambigue*, (Paris, France: Christian Bourgois Édireur, 1990), p. 80. [*Ambiguous Adventure*, translated by Katherine Woods (Portsmouth, NH: Heinemann Educational Books, 1989), p. 68].

[51] Ibid. p. 82 [trans., p. 69, the text actually reads: "Then, he isolates himself and prays"].

spontaneous reaction. It is senseless and vain to open a discussion with a famished stomach. It would be equally senseless and vain, let it be understood [according to the author], to resist the need for religion. But strictly speaking, the religious question is not asked. The author, or more exactly, the *Knight* who is one of his spokesmen, does not really ask himself about the origin and destiny of the human being, and even less does he question about the existence and nature of God. The response in effect is already implied in the formulation of the question: the human being has a "country of origin" beyond the visible world, there exists a personal Being who has brought him into this world and who leads him towards a pre-established destiny. In vain will *Lacroix* try to force the *Knight* to furnish some rational justification for the existence of God. The *Knight*, the father of Samba Diallo, confides in *Lacroix*, "I have sent my son to your school, and I have prayed to God to save us all, you and us," to this *Lacroix* responds in a deliberately provocative manner: "He will save us, if He exists."[52] The *Knight* does not let himself be dragged into the forbidden terrain of debate concerning the essential and is content with pursuing his talk without flinching. God, the essential, is not an object of debate, but only of prayer and adoration. In no case should the believer make him [i.e., God] the object of real questions, that is, of doubting. Regarding

---

[52] Ibid. p. 91 [trans., p. 79].

Pascal, the *Knight* gives his son this advice: "Of the men of the West, he is certainly the most reassuring. But be distrustful even of him. He had doubted."[53] To affirm that religion is the spontaneous reaction of the human being to cosmic fear, as Kane does through the voice of the *Knight*, is to avow that God for the believer is nothing more than a phantom [*fantasme*] deriving from affectivity [i.e., emotionalism], that is to say that he is a product of the heart and of the imagination and keeps the believer at a distance from thought [*pensée*] which is a more elevated form of spirit [i.e., culture].

One thing appears certain: if our intelligence must be shut-up [*s'enfermer*] by the phantom [*fantasme*] of God and the dogmatism of so-called revealed religions, without a doubt it will confirm our defeat. Belief does not oppose itself to knowledge as the depth of interiority to the surface-appearance of exteriority. In reality knowledge and above all knowledge of the essential is more interior and more profound than belief. This latter [i.e., belief] is in effect nothing but the introjection of the wishes and the affirmations of another (great man, prophet, etc.), even when the knowledge that results from it is the result of an active and personal examination of beliefs or of given exterior surface-appearances. Science and modern technology cannot be domesticated but by a people in whom at least the intelligentsia has succeeded in totally

---

[53] Ibid. p. 108 [trans., p. 96].

liberating thought by disengaging it from the shackles of belief [i.e., superstition]. Cheikh Hamidou Kane assigns as a mission to the people of the Third World the re-teaching [*réapprendre*] of faith to the Occident, of bringing to industrial civilization a "supplement for the soul" and has the *Knight* express this prayer: "God, in whom I believe, if we do not succeed, bring about the Apocalypse! Take away from us that liberty of which we shall not have known how to make use. May Thy hand fall heavily, then, upon the great unconscious. May the arbitrary power of Thy will throw out of order the stable course of our laws..."[54] Will someone, gifted with an arbitrary will, hear this fanatic [*fanatique*] and incensed prayer of the *Knight*? It is a question of faith. But the tragic evidence of the present is that certain states, thanks to science and technological civilization, already hold in their hands the secret of the Apocalypse and can, at any moment, put an end to the human adventure.

d. *The Imperialist Occident, Enemy of Thought*

It is not for the cult but for the betrayal of thought [*pensée*, i.e., reason, rationality] that one must reproach Occidental civilization; the Occident is not guilty of the extension and the universalization of reason, but of its criminal limitation. As we say, thought, reason, do not exist:[55] there

---

[54] Ibid. p. 93 [trans., p. 81].
[55] [In other words, "thought" and "reason" do not exist in-themselves, apart from human beings.]

are only [*il n'y a que*] human beings that are thoughtful and reasonable or capable of thought and of reason. It is through thought that the human being affirms his liberty, his power and superiority over all *known* beings. In establishing over the laborers and the peoples of the Third World a system of exploitation and oppression, the Occidental bourgeoisie organized simultaneously the suffocation [*l'étouffement*] of thought and of reason in the vast majority of humanity. The logic of domination directs the international bourgeoisie to ally itself with retrograde forces which it itself had to combat in order to attain its emancipation (fanaticism, superstition, etc.), and to oppose the development of thought amongst its victims because the thinking of the latter cannot but rise-up [*se dresser*] against oppression. The Occident undertook the systematic falsification of the history and the culture of the dominated with the intention of justifying domination. The dehumanization of the dominated peoples which in reality is the result of oppression becomes, in this perspective, the reason for domination and exploitation. Such an enterprise of falsification constitutes a grave violation of scientific objectivity and of reason. Whoever closes his eyes to this reality will suffer a very violent shock, and the international bourgeoisie will pay the price for its blindness, the unrecognized humanity [*l'humanité méconnue*] of dominated peoples will be avenged and already it has begun to be avenged. The recent history of revolutions that are unfolding at the periphery of the capitalist world (Eastern Europe, Asia, Africa, and Latin America) clearly show that the absolute condition for liberation in the modern context is the total emancipation of thought and the appropriation of the scientific spirit. In the end, individualism and the frenzy of accumulation which constitute the inner springs [*resorts intérieurs*] of Occidental imperialism are not unrelated to the Christian religion. The Christian (and Muslim) God is a solitary individual dominating all other beings who must serve him. The identity of divine essence and existence means that the universal, the absolute has the form of an individual. The Christian intends to establish individually an intimate relation with the absolute individuality of God. In God, the human individual enjoys absolute perfection and he himself also becomes somewhat absolute; as such he has no need of any thing or any person other than God. Feuerbach cites an important text of St. Thomas Aquinas: "Frequenting friends is not necessary for happiness [*bonheur*] because the human being possesses in God the total plentitude of his perfection... If then by itself a soul enjoyed God, it would be happy in spite of the absence of a fellow-being [*prochain*] that it could love." "The Christian," comments Feuerbach, has no need of any other self, because, as an individual he is not merely a particular being, but a species being, a universal being, because he "possesses the total plentitude of his perfection in God,"

that is to say in himself.[56] It suffices consequently for the
Christian individual to rid himself of the religious mask in
order to openly set himself up as an absolute being that has
the right to subject the entire world to his unlimited
voracity and to his "arbitrary will," to repeat an expression
of Cheikh Hamidou Kane. This last named, explaining the
significance of his novel, declares: "The conviction of
Samba Diallo is that religious faith (and especially Islam)
constitutes above all a problem which puts in relation, face
to face, the faithful and God,"[57] he prepares ideologically
(mythlogically, to be precise) the terrain for capitalist
individualism, [and] the frenzy of private appropriation
and accumulation characteristic of its [i.e., the capitalist]
mode of production, and the jungle of relations among
classes and peoples that follows. Hence already, under the
direction (by remote control) of the defenders of faith and
of the essentially religious Negro-soul impatient to supply
industrial civilization with a spiritual supplement, our
societies are organized (or disorganized) on this very same
individualistic foundation, destroying, very logically, the
collectivistic traditions wherever they exist. It is
incoherent to disapprove of the actual course of the
majority of our societies while at the same time supporting

---

[56] L. Feuerbach, *L'essence du christianisme*, Maspero, p. 291. [No
other source or reference specification is given.]
[57] Cheikh Hamidou Kane, interview accordée a "Cameroon Tribune,"
du 7 Juillet 1975. [No other source or reference specification is given.]

the ideologies of difference on which, incontestably, this course rests. The complicity between the ideologies of difference and the global system of domination and oppression are today obvious. Oppression, that is to say, let us recall, is the suffocation of the exploited masses, and especially of their thought.

e. *Exorcise the Cult of Difference*
Our opinion is that we have to exorcise the obsession with originality and with difference, that is to say, with tradition, certainly not in order to condemn and reject it as a whole, but in order to judge it after properly studying and examining it with care. Even if one admits the idea of a global progress for humanity, it cannot be said that, in the case of every particular individual or of every particular people, the present is always [or has always been] better than the past; it is thus not rare that the past is preferable to the present, that tradition [at times] is superior to that which is novel. Nevertheless, it is necessary to emphasize that difference, particularity in relation to others, has no value in and of itself, no more than identity in relation to the self and the tradition that defines it. In *Ambiguous Adventure*, Cheikh Hamidou Kane tells us of the tradition of the night of the *Qu'ran*, in the course of which, his "studies completed," the child recites from memory the "Holy Book" in honor of his parents. We comprehend the intense emotion experienced by *Samba Diallo* in fulfilling this tradition, in thinking that he was "in the process of

repeating for his father what the *Knight* [i.e., his father] himself had done for his own father, that which, from generation to generation through the centuries, the sons of the Diallobe had repeated for their fathers..."[58] But if one considers that in general, neither the sons, nor the parents, nor the teachers understood anything of what they were reciting or listening to with such exultation, if one considers above all the extreme brutality of the methods utilized by the teachers in inculcating these enigmatic incantations, how can one not disapprove of such a tradition which is equally delirious and also brutalizing? The incapacity to think the essential observed among adults trained in this manner, we may baptize it with the name of faith, but [in truth] it is nothing more than the terror endured and internalized in infancy.

Let us consider the master and the slave. They are separated by the greatest difference that can exist between beings that are human. The first expresses himself, conceives, thinks, decides, orders, and, in so doing, affirms his generic human identity [*son identité humaine générique*]; while the second, as soon as one goes beyond that which the master considers of no importance, is forbidden from expressing himself, from thinking and from deciding; in other words, his humanity is repressed, suffocated, denied. The slave who would propose to maintain such a difference, and go so far as to glorify it

---

[58] Kane, *L'aventure ambigue*, p. 84 [trans., p. 71 – 72].

reveals nothing but the extremes of brutalization into which slavery has plunged him. Because the relation between the Occident and us is still that of the master and the slave, we have to nourish in regard to all cults of difference and of identity a systematic distrust; without which we run the risk of confirming our servitude. In any case it is vain to want to immobilize tradition and cultural identity, since everything in the universe submits to change. And in passing from nature to culture and history, the rhythm of transformation is accelerated and changes qualitatively. In the cultural world, much more rapidly than in nature, everything is transformed by development or by degradation. In these conditions the problem is not that of knowing if our tradition is going to change or not, change is inevitable, but what changes affect it and how rapidly [is what is at issue]. The question of the nature, the quality, and the orientation [i.e., the direction] of change receives an appreciable clarity [or specification] when the agents which introduce it are defined: merchants or foreign missionaries, nationals, a minority, the masses?

In order to exit [*sortir*] from the dilemma [of choosing] between the ancient and the modern, tradition and revolution, fidelity to self and the imperatives of the present, in order to actively intervene in the process of socio-cultural transformation in progress and to inflect-it [*l'infléchir*] in the right direction, I see only one way: the consciousness of the end [*la conscience de la fin*], of its implications and of its conditions of actualization. The chosen end, the fundamental design, should be the result of a real process of thought, of an examination and of a personal judgment, which takes into account the essential given conditions of historic context. If it is nothing more than the repetition of some traditional dogma more or less skillfully disguised, naturally it cannot be of any help in resolving the dilemma that we have just stated above. Once determined, the end becomes the criterion for the evaluation and judgment of all constituted cultures and of all traditions. All the cultural elements that serve it will be valorized and re-actualized [*réactualisées*], those that are opposed to it will be energetically combated, and nothing will be taken as untouchable *a priori*. It will be, in short, the principle for the construction of the new socio-cultural formation. If this end is, as we have said, liberation not only from the domination of the international bourgeoisie and its indigenous agents, but equally from all traditionalism, be it African, Judeo-Christian or Moslem, it is then in terms of this imperative that everything will be scrutinized and judged. The absolute will no longer be an opaque dogma, a mysterious phantom [*fantasme*], but the concrete human being, his/her needs and aspirations. One thus sees the magnitude of upheavals required to impose [or bring about] such a [radical] transformation.

f. *Revolution as the Condition of all Cultural Renaissance*
Paradoxically, such a revolution rigorously conditions the survival and also the renaissance of tradition and

guarantees difference. Frantz Fanon has insisted with good reason on the idea that revolution as such constitutes an enterprise of cultural creation. To express one's needs and aspirations, to conceive a world such that one finds in it one's accomplishments, to effectively produce such a world, this is the self-same process of cultural creation. By enterprises of such scope, the human being, in one blow affirms his generic identity [*son identité générique*]. In regaining the sense of creative praxis, the revolutionary rejoins all creators, starting with those of his own people, because nothing resembles a creator more than another creator. Traditional artisans are themselves creators. Every great tradition generally arises from a great revolution. Those whose memory has been battered by colonialism are likely to forget this. To say that revolution can be nothing other than the work of audacious human beings, capable of conceiving a different world, and of self-imposed sacrifices in order to realize it, is to recognize that revolutionaries are creators of culture *par excellence*, contrary to the indigenous agents of colonialism and neocolonialism singularly concerned with their immediate interests. From the fact that it is the work of human beings concerned with values, the success of the revolution, despite the upheavals it necessitates, translates itself into the acknowledgment [*reconnaissance*] of the national culture.

The degradation of the traditional culture ensues [*découle*] from domination and notably from the loss of the power of decision. As long as the dominated people have not recovered this power, they are not in a position to revitalize their constituted culture because, as dominated, they are incapable of making decisions. Revolution reverses the colonial relation of forces and places the colonial people anew in a position in which they can exercise choice, concretize and make their choices respected, not only in the political and economic domains but also in that of culture. On the other hand, the neutralization of all traditionalism, that is implied in the revolutionary project as such, plays an important role in the retrieval [*récupération*] of the values of the constituted culture. Traditionalism is the immobilization of tradition by sanctification or by naturalization. Tradition absolutized [*absolutisée*] debilitates and limits. It excludes everything that does not arise from it. In de-sanctifying [*désacralisant*] and in de-naturalizing [*dénaturalisant*] it, the revolution opens it up to all other traditions. One of the most important factors in the cultural renaissance made possible and determined by revolution resides in the role of the masses minimally affected by Westernization. The revolution is above all the promotion of the masses and, by consequence, the promotion of their immured and largely traditional culture. Finally, modern science and technology are generally taken as principally responsible for the destruction of our cultures. If it is true that the scientific spirit cannot root itself except at the detriment of [i.e., by undermining] the supernatural mentality and that the introduction of modern technology necessitates profound transformations at the organizational level of production, of the size of the State, etc..., one must see at the same time that science and technology constitute a powerful trump card [*atout*] in the effort of rediscovering and promoting traditional cultures: researching, transcribing or publishing of the results and their dissemination by the mass media, etc...

CONCLUSION

The resistance that a number of Negro-African intellectuals oppose to science and to reason comes less from the African tradition properly speaking than from the modern African traditionalism of Senghor strongly influenced by colonial racism, as well as Judeo-Christian and Moslem traditionalisms. Because of the strength of cultural nationalism, these last two traditionalisms are presented, more often than not, dressed up in the mask of the former [i.e., cultural nationalism], supported and propped-up by the suspicious thesis of the *incurably* religious Negro.

On the other hand, our broad, even if brief, consideration of the African tradition has convinced us that an important and perhaps dominant current of this tradition has no objections against science as such and is already acquainted, from its most remote antiquity, with the practice of debating on the essential, that is to say philosophy. The Judeo-Christian and Moslem traditions [i.e., the religious traditions that derive from Ibrahim/Abraham] on the contrary can be described as anti-philosophic to the extent that they condemn doubting of and on the absolute and shield it [i.e., the absolute] from all real debate. If this is how things are then the struggle for philosophy, which must oppose colonial racism, the ideological snares of neocolonialism and the dogmatic assaults of Semitic mythologies, is less a borrowing from

European culture than a retrieval of an ancient heritage, a rejuvenating and a revalorizing, and, more profoundly, a reconquest and a reaffirmation of our generic human identity [*de notre identité humaine générique*].

//

IV

Propositions on Cultural Identity:

Detailed Table of Contents

and, for this reason, opens them-up to each other (p. 115).

In the following lines [i.e., in the following numbered sections] we restrict ourselves to presenting our major affirmations in six propositions, in the hope of rendering more visible the compelling direction of our path.

I. The proliferation of ideologies of identity is the symptom of a profound crisis of identity.

Normally, the identity of a people or a civilization is not a problem; it goes without saying. Each people display certain characteristic traits that differentiate it, more or less, from others. Some of these particular traits may be the object of derision or mockery on the part of neighboring peoples, while others may be admired, imitated and may give rise to more or less ephemeral fads. These diverse reactions, by others, provoke fleeting self-conscious glances of consciousness on itself, and are forthwith forgotten, other spiritual concerns [i.e., cultural concerns] having taken their place. The situation, however, becomes qualitatively different when the consciousness of self, of this particularity becomes an obsession, invades the most intimate depths of subjectivity, inspires all literary production, and takes on the dimensions of a veritable ideology. We must then speak of an identity crisis. In a significant manner, it is in the so-called "underdeveloped" countries, the former colonies, that ideologies of identity or of difference proliferate. Other countries, which today are industrialized, Tsarist Russia, Germany of the Romantic era [i.e., of the late 18th and early 19th century] etc., have experienced this same crisis. Since all these cultures displayed the common characteristic of dependence, in the hour of their crisis, on industrialized capitalist countries, we are led to suspect that there is a causal link between this dependence and this crisis.

II. The fundamental cause of the crisis of identity resides in the global system of domination and oppression.

The anguished consciousness of our identity is in reality consciousness of the loss of identity under the dissolving action of exterior forces which we have not been able to control. The principal powers of the center of the capitalist world have allied, in all the societies that they control and dominate, directly or indirectly, with preexisting forces of oppression and inertia. Pushed by the logic of domination, the imperialist powers have battled and destroyed in the societies of the periphery all the *forces – men, institutions, beliefs* – opposed to servitude, that is to say, in general, all that which was most healthy in these societies. With a vengeance [*En revanche*], imperialist Europe, says

Césaire,

> made a firm alliance with all the indigenous
> feudalists who agreed to serve; it devised with them
> obscene plots; rendered their tyranny more effective
> and efficient, and its actions have tended towards
> nothing less than the artificially prolonged survival
> of the most pernicious aspects of the local past...
> colonialist Europe grafted modern abuse onto
> ancient injustice, odious racism onto old
> inequality.[59]

For those who might be tempted to consider Césaire's
assertions excessive, listen to what a great Western
economist, John Kenneth Galbraith, says on the same
question:

> In a country where the land belongs to a small
> minority and is exploited for their benefit, and where
> the apparatus of government serves mainly to
> reinforce these privileges, aid is useless...We have
> no other choice but to keep the Marxist promise of
> ousting the archaic institutions that block progress.

As Galbraith is obliged to note:

> By a curious deformation of intelligence, those who
> consider themselves to be the most experienced and
> subtle in matters of foreign policy have regularly

---

[59] Aimé Césaire, *Discours sur le colonialism* (Paris, France: Présence
Africaine, 1955), p. 22 [*Discourse on Colonialism*, p. 24. As already
noted in footnote 45, Towa's rendition, of this quote, varies slightly
from the original and from the standard translation.]

recommended the support of the most disgusting dictators. The consequences have always been disastrous – except for the architects of these policies who get promoted or retire with a reputation for having very subtle views.[60]

The alliance between the Western powers and all the oppressive and retrograde forces leads to the formation, under their direction, of a truly global system of domination.

***

Western imperialism finds one of its most elaborate ideological expressions in the Hegelian philosophy of history according to which the modern civilization of Europe constitutes the universal synthesis of all the values produced by humanity in the course of its long history. The Occident is thus proclaimed the Absolute of the world in front of whom all other peoples are without rights. In it *Weltgeist* [*l'Esprit du monde*] is completely developed and determined: "the principle is realized and, as a consequence, time is complete." The other civilizations have nothing of value to offer which Europe, universal heritage of humanity, does not already posses, as a surpassed moment of the historic development of Spirit, integrated in it as a particular determination. In other

---

[60] John Kenneth Galbraith, *Les conditions du développement économique*, Nouveaux horizons, 1964, pp. 56 – 59. [No other source or reference specification is given.]

words, in front of European civilization, other civilizations and peoples are without value and can therefore be reduced by it to the condition of mere instruments. Thus the Christian Occident, according to Hegel, "does not have anything exterior [to it] in an absolute sense but only relatively which in itself has been overcome and regarding which it suffices to render manifest that it has already been overcome."[61] Under cover of this absolutization [*absolutisation*] of itself, the West indulges, with a clear conscience, in the *destruction of other civilizations throughout the world*. In itself, enslavement is fatal to all cultural creativity. The cultural world results from man's self-conscious awareness of his needs and aspirations, from knowledge of the given reality and the transformations of this objective reality allowing for the satisfaction of needs. We see then that this *process of cultural creation is merged with free praxis*. The identity of cultural creation and free praxis helps us to understand why an attempt [*atteinte*] on the liberty of a people constitutes an attempt [i.e., an attack] on the culture of that people. To enslave a people means to restrict them to an activity that does not arise from their proper needs, but that of another, for an end which is not theirs, but that of another. The enslaved people are inserted, as an

---

[61] Hegel, *Leçons sur la philosophie de l'histoire*, Nouvelle edition trad., J. Giblin, 1945, pp. 313 – 314. [No other source or reference specification is given.]

instrument, into a practical process whose motivations and goals remain alien and even unknown to them. The culture thus produced is therefore not theirs but that of another. The enslavement of a people dries up its culture at its source.

This was precisely the experience that the peoples of Africa had with the slave trade, and then colonization. Our defeat in clashing with the West was translated into cultural devastation. The invaders, notably the missionaries, indulged in pure cultural vandalism, destroying or pillaging works of art, making war on our religions and beliefs. Our leaders and political institutions became mere cogs in the colonial administrative machinery, our languages, reservoirs of our cultural patrimony, were forbidden, economic life was disrupted, craft-industry asphyxiated, etc. More damaging than this destruction of our constituted culture was the loss of the *historic initiative*. In preventing us in this manner from the "dialectic of needs," colonialism culturally sterilized us making it impossible for us to create. And yet, one may object, it was defeated Greece which civilized triumphant Rome. This example does not in the least contradict our thesis; on the contrary it confirms it completely, since Roman conquest certainly led to the death of Greek culture. A culture, we maintain, is a structured dynamic ensemble of institutions, of functions, of conceptions, etc. In disintegrating this totality or in immobilizing it, conquest literally kills it; for immobilization and disintegration mean death. The elements set loose by this disintegration can very well be synthesized in foreign centers and enter in the composition of new dynamic totalities, without however reconstituting the original totality. The modern world, after Rome, can very well nourish itself on the elements set loose by Greek culture; this does not diminish, in the least, its considerable difference from the Greek world. Today, one can certainly learn Greek or Latin in modern high schools [*les lycées modernes*], but this does not make, Greek and Latin, any less "dead" as languages, that is to say languages that do not develop anymore. The conquest of Greece disrupted not only its culture, it put the Greek people, *deprived of historic initiative*, in a situation in which it was impossible for them to restructure and develop their culture.

If conquerors necessarily destroy the culture of the conquered and enslaved people, do they at least replace it with their own? Léopold Sédar Senghor responds in the affirmative in order to rehabilitate colonization. We read in *Nation et voie africaine du socialism*:

> Let us stop vituperating colonialism and Europe… To be sure, the conquerors sowed ruin in their path, but also ideas and techniques… Europe did not lose by the Roman conquest… On the plane of History, the bloody event is elevated to the level of an

Advent: it is Revolution.[62]

But this is nothing but an illusion which Césaire proposed to call "the illusion of Deschamps," the name of a governor of colonies who defended it at the Sorbonne in 1956. Modern European civilization is not the work of Gallo-Romans bent under the yoke of Rome chanting the glory and the beauty of the "Metropolis," it is the creation of Barbarians having conquered, in their turn, superb Rome. It is free Japan, and not colonized India which has drawn on the best part of European civilization. In fact, in the colonies, colonialist Europe necessarily practiced what Malinowski called "selective giving." It exported Christianity in its most conservative version, pornographic films, but never the instruments of physical power, the principles of industrial civilization, as testified by the miserable state of technical education in all the colonized or neocolonized countries. The reason is that the colonialists or neocolonialists are not quite so insane as to stir-up [*susciter*] a rival civilization whose first concern would be to finish with domination: colonialism has no taste for suicide.

---

[62] Léopold Sédar Senghor, *Nation et voie africaine du socialisme*, Présence Africaine, p. 109 et suivants. [*On African Socialism* (New York: Frederick A. Praeger, Pub., 1964), pp. 80 – 81.]

III. The societies affected by the crisis of identity can overcome this crisis only by becoming once again centers of conscious self-movement and transformation, thereby eradicating domination and oppression.

The crisis of identity on the level of literature and of ideology in general is the consciousness of the process of disintegration unfolding in the dominated countries as an effect of domination. It cannot be resolved either by maintaining our present situation or by restoring the past. Our present identity is characterized by feebleness, domination direct or indirect, [and] the humiliation and degradation of our cultures. In this condition, the cult of our present identity and of the difference from Europe signifies the maintenance, overtly or covertly, of our powerlessness and of our dependence. The greatest actual difference between the Occident and Africa is that between the master and the slave. The difference between a free person and an enslaved person is, in our view, the greatest conceivable difference between beings that are human: it is the difference between he who exercises the power of initiative and creation and he who is deprived of this and who, because of this, remains on a natural sub-human level of existence. This difference must be abolished; the human being degraded below humanity [*l'homme ravalé au-dessous de l'homme*] must negate this downfall and regain his power of initiative and creativity, that is to say, his generic human identity. Certainly, a number of Africans profit from our actual condition and struggle to maintain it. Thus our aspirations for identity have never been identical, no more today than in the past. The past is not more homogeneous [than the present]. The past is a process; its visage changes in accordance with epochs and classes. Which period, which aspect of the past is to be restored? One must choose because the diverse aspects it puts-on [*revêtus*] in accordance with epochs and classes are not at all compatible. Our view [*vision*] of the past cannot be uniformly optimistic: we were defeated by Europe, in a massive clash with it, in which we ended up at the bottom. Our historic defeat shows that there was in our past identity, in our particular being as it arises [*provient*] from the past, something insufficient, a lacuna which was the cause of our defeat and which explains our persistent incapacity to reverse this defeat. This is why our specific identity, past or present, has to be revolutionized. To what extent? To the exact extent required for the affirmation of our generic human identity, the power of conception, of signification, of thought and of implementation. Nothing, *a priori*, in our particular culture is to be considered untouchable. We do not uphold any element of our constituted culture or the totality of this constituted culture as having absolute value, but the generic human identity, source of all constituted culture. Human generic identity, as the constituting activity of all culture, is elevated above all particular cultures because it engenders them all. Our fundamental design will be an auto-centric Africa having in its own self its centers of conception, decision-making, and implementation in the totality of its spheres of essential activity: political, economic and spiritual [i.e., cultural]; a fraternal Africa, *respectful of this same principle of auto-centration [auto-centration] as it pertains to its own institutions and those of other peoples.*

IV. It is this fundamental goal – Transcendence – which determines the attitude regarding traditions and the choice of means, some of which may even be taken from the dominator himself.

The final goal provides us with a criterion of evaluation for all constituted cultures, for all traditions, for all particular identities. We are in effect interested in all traditions, in all constituted cultures, because they are all in principle at our disposal. The status of the cultural, relative to the psycho-organic hereditary structure, is that of exteriority. Once produced, all cultural elements become detachable from their producers and are available to whoever can appropriate them. It is because all cultural creations are at the mercy of whoever wants to appropriate them that a particular legislation is necessary for the protection of the property rights of intellectual producers. The German or French person who has studied Greek language and literature has thereby appropriated a number of elements of this culture which he could teach even to a Greek person. The fact of being Greek does not automatically confer upon him [i.e., a Greek person] the possession of Greek culture. This last [i.e., Greek culture] is exterior even to him [i.e., a person who happens to be Greek] and he also will not be able to appropriate it without great cost and effort. Christianity was taken from the Jews by the Europeans who then turned it against the Jews themselves. We can make the same observation regarding Marxism born on Germanic soil it next became Sovietic and then Chinese. The Chinese have turned it against the Soviets who themselves did not hesitate to turn it against the Germans who had produced it. To be sure, in changing hands and countries borrowed cultural elements undergo, more or less, profound modifications in accordance with the needs of the borrowing milieu.

The appropriation of constituted culture [*de la culture constituée*] may take place passively and without reflection, through chance encounters, of birth or conquest, or actively, as a function of needs and aspirations. We conceive the final goal, that is to say autocentration [*autocentration*], not as an utopia that can most certainly remain a pure ideal, but as a project to concretize. A revolutionary project differs from a dream or an utopia insofar as it contains within its conception the outline for the conditions and the process of its actualization. The preliminary determination of these conditions is of decisive importance. It is only in the light of a sufficient elucidation of our fundamental design and in view of its actualization that we can orient ourselves in the labyrinth of traditions, whether our own proper traditions, or those of the Jews, the Arabs or the Europeans. All that which, in these cultural traditions, can be inserted into the world we are proposing to institute and into the process of its actualization will be conserved and all that which blocks or is in-the-way [*gênerait*] of this process will be coldly discarded and if need be resolutely combated.

V. Only approximate equality of material power can guarantee the conscious self-movement of peoples and at the same time the liberty of choice among traditions.

Neither religion, nor ethics or the law can suffice to assure among human beings equality and fraternity. Historical experience shows that those who have at their disposal sufficient superiority on the physical plane cannot long resist the temptation of abusing it to dominate and exploit the feebler ones. Peace and fraternity cannot be established among human beings without a relative equality on the level of material power. If this is so, it takes on a lofty moral value and its generalization ought to be sought in so far as it is the essential condition for a reconciled humanity. Unequal material power among classes and among peoples makes domination possible, the oppression of man by man and in their train the destruction of values and the sterilization of cultures. But physical power, decisive for the destiny of our world, is hidden in the intimacy of matter. The cudgel [*trique*] with which the Occident holds the peoples on their knees is none other than the energy of the molecule and of the atom captured and tamed by modern technology. Industrial civilization is based on science and the application of science to productive work. It is born from the union of theoretic knowledge and artisanal practice. Thus, knowledge becomes practical and artisanal-crafts become theoretic, in other words, artisanal practice becomes technology. It has resulted, just as Bacon and Descartes had wished, in a revolutionary extension of the power of man over nature. The technological revolution led to certain social and political transformations: the destruction of feudal structures and the mobility of labor-power, the formation of large national states that constitute the economic spaces that correspond to the unprecedented increase in production. On the other hand, it seems quite clear that science and technology could not have taken root and developed without the ruin of the magico-religious mentality. Supernaturalism is a form of subjectivism which pretends to directly submit nature to the impatience and the arbitrariness of desire, while technology grounds its action on knowledge of and respect for determinism, that is to say on the objective regularity of natural processes. A people definitively cannot tame the scientific and technical spirit if it is not able to generate an intelligentsia free of all magico-religions allegiance. The conquest of science and of modern technology, the secret power of industrial civilization, thus imposes for the most part, profound transformations on the cultural traditions of peoples. On the other hand, it constitutes the indispensable base for the power of decision and of actualization; in other words, it grounds liberty, creativity, the principle for the formation of particular cultures. Furthermore, power makes it possible to resist all cultural impositions, it provides the means for studying and revalorizing that which merits to be [*celles qui méritent de l'être*]. The danger to our cultures comes not from industrialization but from imperialism. Imperialism condemns our cultures to disintegration and death, industrialization imposes on us their revolutionizing as the only means to assure survival and development.

VI. The collapse of the global system of domination would liberate the creativity of peoples and multiply the creative centers of cultures conscious of their limitations and, for this reason, would open them up to each other.

Such an eventuality would constitute a considerable revolution. In the periphery the identity crisis, in the center, the Occident's pompous self-consciousness bloated to the point of absolutisation [*l'absolutisation*] and self-adoration, would disappear more or less rapidly, these two connected phenomena being nothing more than the ideological aspects of the same system of domination. Consumer civilization would also undergo profound transformations because its current crassness is tied to the system of domination and its need to manipulate the masses. Marcuse has explained how the system creates, as it were, a new nature and stimulates needs such that their satisfaction reproduces monopoly capitalism. If the system of domination were to be abolished, the peoples would become conscious of their needs and their real aspirations, [and would] express them in art and in theoretic reflection and by working to satisfy them [i.e., their needs], that is to say, by affirming their generic human identity and their creativity: and he who says creativity says active spirit, says innovation, diversification. If the collapse of the global system of domination is conditioned by the relative equality of material power among peoples or groups of peoples, equality of power which itself depends on the generalization of industrial civilization, then those who struggle to establish concretely these conditions have a better chance of accomplishing much more for the advent of a reconciled humanity and for a spiritualized world than those beautiful souls who are satisfied with moral preaching, more than those consumed by waiting for the arrival of a Hero, a Messiah, charged with bringing us a "supplement for the soul" (*"supplément d'âme"*) and installing on earth, by mysterious ways, the kingdom of the Spirit.

//

V

A Note on Towa and Serequeberhan

Marcien Towa is from the village of Endama, located 60 km from Yaoundé, the capital of Cameroun. He secured his Baccalaureate in philosophy in 1955 and went on to peruse higher studies starting from 1957, first at Caen and then at the Sorbonne. In 1959 he obtained his *licence en philosophie* and in 1960 the *Diplôme d'Etudes Supérieures* in the same discipline with a dissertation on Bergson and Hegel. After teaching for a year at the *Ecole Normale Supérieure* of Yaoundé, he went on to pursue studies in *pscycho-pédagogie* thanks to a UNESCO scholarship which took him to Paris, London, Birmingham, Geneva, Moscow, Leningrad, and Baku. Towa is one of the "founding fathers" of the contemporary discourse of African philosophy.

Tsenay Serequeberhan is originally from Eritrea and presently lives and works in the USA. He secured his B.A., in political science from the University of Massachusetts (Boston) in 1979 and his M.A., and Ph.D., in philosophy, from Boston College in 1982 and 1988 respectively. He has taught in various institutions of higher learning and is presently professor of philosophy at Morgan State University. His research, focused on social and political issues, is aimed at exploring the intersecting concerns of African/Africana and Continental European philosophy. He is the author of four books and numerous scholarly articles and, in Anglophone African philosophy, a pioneer proponent of the practice of philosophy as a concrete hermeneutic of the African situation.